Derbyshire
Edited by Steve Twelvetree

Young Writers

First published in Great Britain in 2005 by:
Young Writers
Remus House
Coltsfoot Drive
Peterborough
PE2 9JX
Telephone: 01733 890066
Website: www.youngwriters.co.uk

All Rights Reserved

© Copyright Contributors 2005

SB ISBN 1 84602 153 7

Foreword

Young Writers was established in 1991 and has been passionately devoted to the promotion of reading and writing in children and young adults ever since. The quest continues today. Young Writers remains as committed to the fostering of burgeoning poetic and literary talent as ever.

This year's Young Writers competition has proven as vibrant and dynamic as ever and we are delighted to present a showcase of the best poetry from across the UK. Each poem has been carefully selected from a wealth of *Playground Poets* entries before ultimately being published in this, our thirteenth primary school poetry series.

Once again, we have been supremely impressed by the overall high quality of the entries we have received. The imagination, energy and creativity which has gone into each young writer's entry made choosing the best poems a challenging and often difficult but ultimately hugely rewarding task - the general high standard of the work submitted amply vindicating this opportunity to bring their poetry to a larger appreciative audience.

We sincerely hope you are pleased with our final selection and that you will enjoy *Playground Poets Derbyshire* for many years to come.

Contents

Arboretum Primary School
Jibral Peeno (8)	1
Rezza Bashir	1
Nadia Afzal (8)	1
Amar Hussain (8)	2
Demi Simpson (8)	2
Abbas Sadique (8)	2
Daniel Pitter (9)	3
Arusa Hussain (8)	3
Shahzaib Mahmood (8)	3
Zeeshan Khan (8)	4
Sanaah Sultan (10)	4
Maryam Iqbal (8)	4
Asim Mahmood (8)	5
Kaleem Ali (8)	5
Alisha Rashid (8)	5
Nafeesa Saghir (8)	6

Ashgate Primary School
Tana-Leigh Gannon (8)	6
Joe Winfield (8)	6
Archie Attwood (9)	7
Daisy Riley (7)	7
Alex Bird (8)	7
Michael Bird (9)	8
Alix Laxton (7)	8
Lauren Jenns (8)	8
Hellen Biete (8)	9
Zoe Smith (9)	9
Zoe Hanrahan (9)	9
Samantha Whitby (8)	10
Stephanie Brown (9)	10
Demi Hughes (7)	11
Kathleen Harty (8)	11
Nico Begni (8)	11
Ryan Lambert (8)	12
Callum Redfern (8)	12
Kayleigh Fletcher (9)	13
Joab Coulson (7)	13

Sophie Harrison (9)	13
Liam Heldreich (8)	14
Mitchell Atterbury (8)	14
Bethany Lawrence (9)	14

Asterdale Primary School

Annie Horsley (8)	15
Megan Cartwright (8)	15
Hollie Miller (8)	15
Joe Cokayne (8)	16
Tamara Thompson (8)	16
Katrina Thompson (8)	16
Kieran Eames (9)	17
Ben Cooper (8)	17
George Lawrenson (9)	17
Thomas Erskine (8)	18
Zak Merrin (8)	18
Jemma Hawksworth (8)	18
David Oakley (9)	19
Lewis Dickens (9)	19
Elle Ford (9)	19
Kane Jordan (9)	20
Jyoti Nazran (8)	20
Siobhan Sutton (9)	20
Aimee Miller (9)	21
Jessica Woods (10)	21
Lauren Secker (9)	21
Carly Bates (9)	22
Becky Painter (10)	22
Ryan Mason (9)	23
Rebecca Stainforth (9)	23
Nyasha Chabaya (9)	23
Gemma Jackson (10)	24
Stuart Morris (9)	24
Annie Sheldon (9)	25
Laura Colder (9)	25
Jade Cousins (10)	25
Thomas Cox (10)	26
Emily Tomlinson (10)	26
Daniel Page (10)	26
Lauren Spencer (9)	27

Sam Wilson (10)   27
Hayley Binfield (9)   27
Jason Carpenter (9)   28
Lauren Cook (10)   28
Ryan Sheldon (10)   28
Jack Cartwright (8)   29
Ryan Bailey (9)   29

Bradley CE Primary School
Alex Monro-Jones (9)   29
Maisie Forton (11)   30
Daniel Yeomans (9)   30
Rebecca Woodward (10)   31
Amy Mason (9)   31
Samantha Bebbington (9)   31
Scott Galvin (11)   32
Rian Galvin (8)   32
Chris Bellamy (9)   32
Laurel Stone (8)   33
Rachel Relihan (10)   33
Chloe Bellamy (11)   34
Natalie Campbell-Lyons (10)   34
Sam Bigland (10)   34
Thomas Weston (8)   35
Maria Webb (8)   35

Brassington Primary School
Nicola Hartley (7)   35
Josephine Gilbert (10)   36
Owen Wilkinson (10)   36
Thomas Ball (9)   37
Chenma Hayhurst (8)   37
Grace Charlton (10)   38
Daisy Howstan (9)   38

Granby Junior School
Annabel Yau (10)   39
Chloe Timmis (10)   39
Anya Holland (9)   40
Laurie Plant (9)   40
Lucy Detheridge (10)   41

Abigail Sisson (10)   41
Sophie Barratt (9)   42
Carly Baker (10)   42
Georgina Thornley (10)   43

Hilton Primary School
Jade Chan (9)   43
Jemma Webster (9)   44
Thomas Reardon (10)   44
Josie McCormick (10)   45
William Hardie (9)   45
Alice Francis (10)   46
Dan Hicklin (10)   46
Megan Russell (10)   46
Alex Millington (10)   47
Charlotte Harlow (9)   47
Thomas Brown (10)   48
Mostafa Sallam (9)   48
George Bloor (9)   49
Naomi Murfin (9)   49
Alexandra Robinson (9)   50
Alice Genders (10)   50

Hollinsclough CE Primary School
Tiffany Belfield (8)   51
Sara Bradley (9)   51
Julie Mellor (11)   52
Joe Middleton (10)   52
Molly Hadfield (8)   52
Ella Middleton (9)   53
Georgiana Oddy (11)   53
Zachary Ralph Jupp (10)   54
Shannon Belfield (9)   54
Harry Johnson (11)   55
Georgina Ball (7)   55
Samantha Fletcher (8)   56
Joshua Slack (10)   56
Jamie Beresford-Cook (11)   56
Max Hertzog (8)   57
Luke Keeling (10)   57
Matthew Bradley (8)   57

Mickleover Primary School
Hannah Wagg (9)	58
Lydia Roworth (9)	59
Alex Nelson (9)	60
Keely Glynn (9)	61
Thomas Robson (9)	62
Chris Mann (10)	63
Matthew Twigg (9)	64
Helen Perry (9)	65
Sam Aulsebrook (10)	66
Jamie Turner (10)	67
Georgina Barker (10)	68
Natasha Payne (10)	69
Kiran Shanker (9)	70
Emily Reader (9)	71
Katie Yeomans (9)	72
Alec James (10)	73
Alexander James Suckling (9)	74
Alice Southall (9)	75
Tom Foster (9)	76
Rhiannon Smallman (9)	77
Danny Cunningham (9)	78
Mollie Garratt (9)	79
Ryan Skidmore (10)	80

Oakthorpe Primary School
Sanchez Frank (9)	80
Connor Cannon (9)	81
David Ashworth (9)	81
Anna Southerd (10)	82
Callum Lennon (10)	82
Leah Commons (10)	83
Olivia Bozeat (10)	83
Kane Marriott (10)	84
Kathryn Adams (11)	84
Jordan Barry (11)	85
Sabrina Collins (10)	85

Old Hall Junior School
George Dixon (9)	86
Tom Mounsey (10)	87

Katie Swift (10)	87
Amy Marie Duffy (11)	88
Laura Harrison (11)	88
Lorna Stone (10)	89
Anna Stephanie Casper (9)	89
Anna Elizabeth Griffiths (10)	90
Ruth Rastrick (10)	90
Emma Dewick (11)	91
Taylor Spencer (10)	91
Jade Wong (11)	92
Jake Armitage (9)	92
Charlotte Eyre (11)	93
James Marriott (10)	93
Katie Dargue (10)	94
Mollie Varley (11)	94
Ruth Rastrick (10)	95
Bethany Herrick (10)	95
Chloe Taylor (10)	96
Peta Forder (10)	96
Lorna Stone & Daisy Stopher (10)	97
Ashton Hurst (9)	97
Kathryn Borrell (11)	98
Laurie Woodgate (9)	98
Ellie Simpson (10)	99
Jack McKinley (9)	99
Megan Biggs (8)	100
Joshua Mouncer (10)	100
David Smith (10)	101
Ethan Alexander Iles (9)	101
Rowen Bell (10)	102
Adam Sharp (9)	103
Poppy Whittaker (9)	103
Ellie Burroughs (10)	104
Benjamin Warsop (10)	104
Amy Rees (9)	105
Zoë Ball (10)	105
Laura Maycock (10)	106
Stephanie Willett (9)	106
Samantha Harcourt (10)	107
Jasmine Hardy (9)	107
Olivia Doyle (9)	108
Jonathon Dunn (10)	108

Charlotte Machin (9)	109
Robyn Canner (9)	109
Abbie Layton (9)	110
Robert Hepworth (9)	110
Georgina Layton (10)	111
Jack Wilson (9)	111
Amy Carty (8)	112
Molly Cannon (9)	112
Jack Morton (8)	113
Jessica Dolling (10)	113
Emily Mason (8)	114
Daniel Lobar (9)	114
Eleanor Haughey (8)	115
Tyler Bonser (10)	115
Eleanor Middleton (9)	116
Edmund Austin (9)	116
Harry Large (9)	117
Emily Calladine (9)	118
Jacob Smith (9)	118
Niccòlo Ebong (8)	119
Oliver Naughton (8)	119
Nicola Hill (8)	120

Redhill Primary School

Matthew Parker (11)	120
Holly Riley (10)	121
Siobhan Wenham (11)	121
Katie Louise Tatam (7)	122
Jack Thompson (10)	122
Laura Clough (11)	123
Kirsty Dakin (10)	123
Hannah Brown (7)	124
Sophie Webster (10)	124
Josie Smith (8)	124
Jamie Fenwick (11)	125
Vanessa Radford (11)	125
Ellie May Lawson (8)	126
Elinor Hardcastle (8)	126
Phoebe Garside (8)	126
Haydn Bowley (11)	127
Jack Hodgkinson (8)	127

St Joseph's Catholic Primary School, Derby
Danielle Mortimer (11)	127
Natalie Bentley (11)	128
Eleanor Balwako (10)	128
Otis Gratton (10)	129
Alice Iddon (10)	129
Mark Durkan (10)	130
Joe Koscinski (11)	130
Paige Kathryn Smith (11)	131
Jacob Rollinson (10)	131
Bethany Masters (10)	132
Victoria Wyatt (11)	132
Fawn Quick (11)	132
Lauren Finnegan (10)	133
James Durkan (10)	133
Emma Joyce (10)	134

St Peter & St Paul School, Chesterfield
Chloe Knowles (10)	134
Georgia Stansbury (9)	135
James Davies (10)	135
Sam Mather (9)	136
Katherine Parkin (9)	137
Laura Singleton (9)	138
Alexander Hodgkinson (9)	138
Rebecca Bayliff (9)	139
Callum Howie (10)	139
Lewis Spencer (10)	140
Siân Carter (9)	140
Richard Berry (10)	141
Simon Meikle (8)	141
Guy Swales (9)	142
Mary-Beth Owen (9)	142
James Rowland (10)	143
Charlotte Adams (10)	143
Edward Richardson (9)	144
Bryony Hill (8)	144
Erin Hawker (9)	145
James Watson (9)	145
Ellie Birch (9)	146
Amber Richardson (9)	146

Laura Hattersley (9)   147
Sara Sinclair (8)   148

St Wystan's School, Repton
Patrick Field (9)   148
Peter Bralesford (9)   149
David Boiling (9)   149
Aimee Holder-Spinks (10)   150
Richard Sommerville (9)   150
Robert Egan (11)   151
Oliver Startin (10)   151
Sophie Donoghue (11)   152
Liam Rhatigan (10)   152
Holly Twells (11)   153
Eleanor Harrison (9)   153
Oliver Richards (10)   154
Chloe Marshall (10)   154
Harriet Boyles (11)   155
Philippa Stazicker (9)   155
Thomas Jones (12)   156
Holly Wright (9)   156
Emily Hammond (11)   157
Charlotte Downs (9)   157
Victor Scattergood (11)   158
Tristan Griffiths (10)   159
Matthew Cort (11)   160
Hollie Strong (10)   160
Jessica Storey (10)   161

Thornsett Primary School
George Lee (9)   161
Olivia Ashley (10)   162
Owen Baldwin (11)   163
Iain Barr (9)   164
Kieran Hopley (10)   164
Poppy Philligreen (9)   165
Nicola Kemp (10)   165
Reece Jennings (7)   166
Bethany Finch (9)   166
Emilie Lee (7)   166

Daniella Gabbott (7) 167
Katy Waddell (11) 167

Wigley Primary School
Olivia Haslam (10) 167
Kate Walker (10) 168
Jack Boughey (10) 168
Rebecca Hannon (10) 168

The Poems

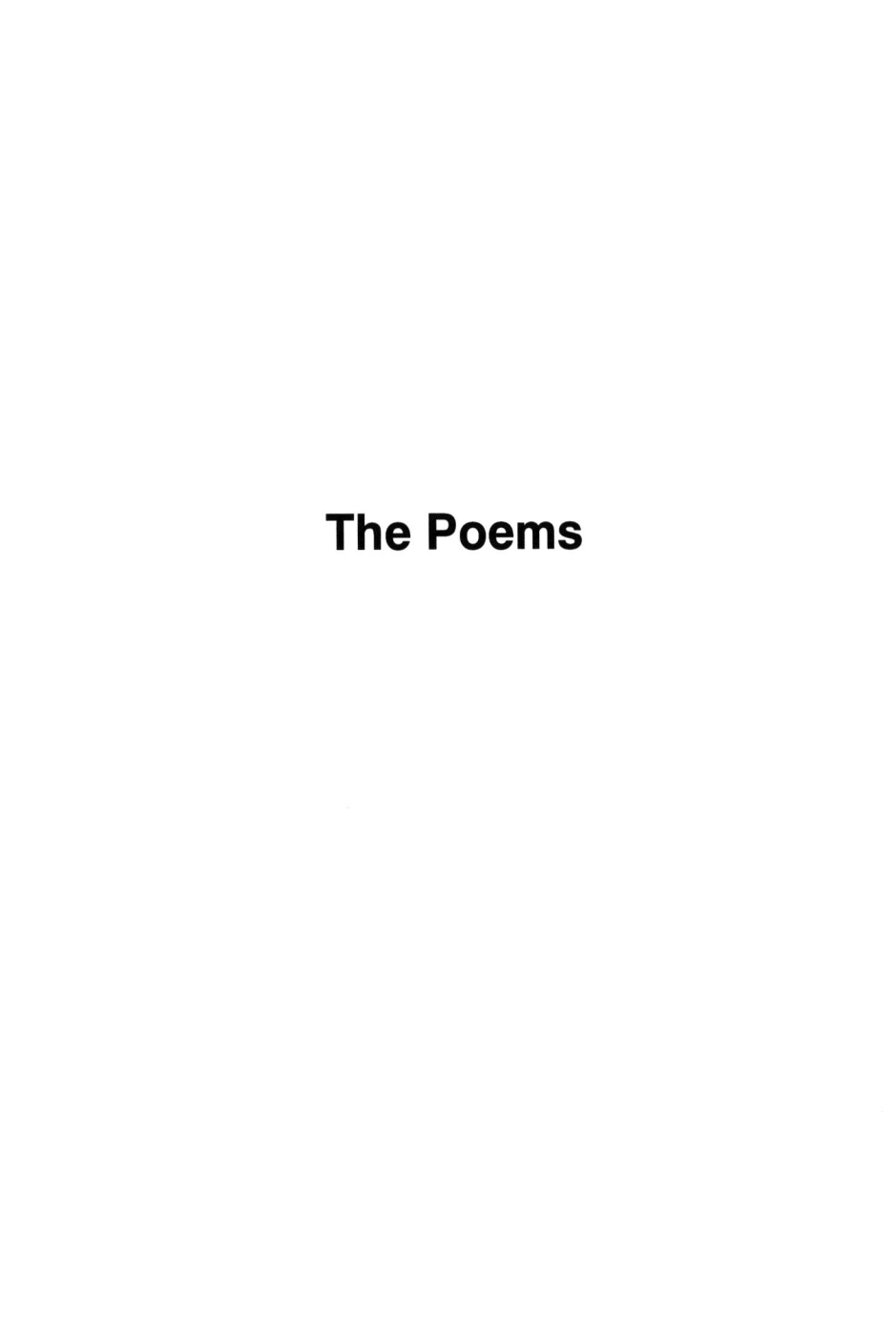

Miss Allen

She's as comfortable as a bed
She's as nice as a soft chair
Sweet as a deer
Kind as a panda
She is as soft as a rose
And as bright as a sunflower.

Jibral Peeno (8)
Arboretum Primary School

Miss Allen

She's as bouncy as a bed
She's a gentle, kind deer
She's a nice teacher
She's as nice as roses
She's a bed full of roses
She's as comfortable as cotton wool.

Rezza Bashir
Arboretum Primary School

Miss Allen

She's a beautiful, bouncy chair
She's a lovely, elegant, comfortable sofa
She's a gorgeous deer
She's as pretty as a flamingo
She's as glamorous as a rose
She's as gorgeous as a sunflower
She's as hot as a bowl of tea each and every day.

Nadia Afzal (8)
Arboretum Primary School

Mrs Stanton

A comfortable, big chair
A nice, soft, vast bed
Big as a lion
Sweet as a deer
Nice as a puppy
And a bed of roses
A hot chocolate drink
On a winter's day.

Amar Hussain (8)
Arboretum Primary School

My Sister

She is a sticky floor
And an open door
She is a dandelion
And ivy
She is as sour as a lemon
She is my sister and a cuddly teddy bear.

Demi Simpson (8)
Arboretum Primary School

Miss S Williams

She's as shiny as scissors
She's as bouncy as a bed
She's tall as a chair
She is jolly like a hyena
She's soft like a lion
She smells like roses
She's as pretty as a sunflower
She's smooth like hot chocolate
On a cold winter's day!

Abbas Sadique (8)
Arboretum Primary School

Miss Williams

She is bouncy as a bed
She is as bouncy as a chair
She's a kangaroo
She's as fast as a lion
She smells like a dandelion
She's like a flower
A round face like an apple
And likes apples.

Daniel Pitter (9)
Arboretum Primary School

The Sun

The sun is like a ball of sunshine
Flying round the world
Showing off its glorious beauty
Everywhere it goes
The sun is like an attractive jewel
That sends wishes to me.

Arusa Hussain (8)
Arboretum Primary School

Miss S Williams

She's as bouncy as a sofa
She's as bouncy as a cushion
She's as soft as a lion
She's as furry as a monkey
She's as sweet as a rose
She's as bright as a daffodil
She's as nice as hot chocolate
She's like a sweet cup of tea.

Shahzaib Mahmood (8)
Arboretum Primary School

Miss Williams

She's as comfy as a bed
She's as fast as a lion
She's as funny as a monkey
She smells like a rose.

Zeeshan Khan (8)
Arboretum Primary School

My Mum

She's as comfy as my bed
As loyal as a book
She's as happy as a kitten
As strict as a swan
She's as sweet as a rose
As beautiful as a daisy
She is as lovely as hot chocolate
On a cold winter's day.

Sanaah Sultan (10)
Arboretum Primary School

Miss Sarah Williams

She's as bouncy as a chair
As strong as a bed
She's as beautiful as a peahen
As sweet as a deer
She smells like roses
As pretty as daffodils
She's a juicy strawberry.

Maryam Iqbal (8)
Arboretum Primary School

Mr Harris

He is as cuddly as a teddy bear
He is as soft as cotton wool
He is as sweet as a deer
He is as lovely as a bird
He smells like a bed of roses
He is as nice as a sunflower
He's as soft as a marshmallow.

Asim Mahmood (8)
Arboretum Primary School

Miss Williams

Miss Williams is a bed full of roses
She is like a tiger
She is rosy like an apple
She is a jumping spring
She is a comfy bed.

Kaleem Ali (8)
Arboretum Primary School

Miss Williams

Miss Williams is a gorgeous chair
She's a bouncy, bright bed
She's as fast as a hare
She's a sporting giraffe
She's full of roses
Glows like a daffodil
She's as lovely as sugar.

Alisha Rashid (8)
Arboretum Primary School

Miss Allen

She's as bouncy as soft fur
Like roses in a bed
She's a comfortable bed
She's a sweet rose
She smells of roses
She's as gorgeous as mirrors.

Nafeesa Saghir (8)
Arboretum Primary School

Love

Love is as red as a rose
It sounds like birds singing sweetly to me
It tastes like a delicious chocolate cake
It smells like a bunch of flowers
It looks like a dream come true
It reminds me of when I had my first birthday.

Tana-Leigh Gannon (8)
Ashgate Primary School

Anger

Anger is as hot as a volcano
It is as red as lava
It sounds like a volcano erupting
It tastes horrible like salty water
It smells like horrible smoke
It looks like lightning
It reminds me of when I punched the wall.

Joe Winfield (8)
Ashgate Primary School

Darkness

Darkness is as black as a black widow
Darkness sounds like somebody walking behind you
Darkness tastes like gum without any taste
Darkness smells like ice-cold air
Darkness looks like a black devil
Darkness reminds me of when I was sleeping in the dark.

Archie Attwood (9)
Ashgate Primary School

Love

Love is pink, as pink as a rose
It sounds like magic waving about
Love tastes like red jelly
It smells like blueberries
Love looks like presents on Christmas Day
It reminds me of when I had my first boyfriend.

Daisy Riley (7)
Ashgate Primary School

Fear

Fear is as dark as a witch's cat
Fear sounds like a werewolf's howl
Fear tastes like forty lemons put together
Fear smells like mouldy milk
Fear looks like a hungry monster
Fear reminds me of when my brother went through the window.

Alex Bird (8)
Ashgate Primary School

Darkness

Darkness is as black as the blazing night sky
It reminds me of a black building
And when I go to my bed and lie down my sweet little head
Darkness smells like chocolate cake
It tastes sour
It sounds like an owl hooting in the moonlit sky.

Michael Bird (9)
Ashgate Primary School

Love

Love is as red as blood
Love sounds like trumpets singing in silence
Love tastes like fresh flowers
Love smells like beautiful roses
Love looks like red lava in the shape of a love heart
Love reminds me of red nail varnish.

Alix Laxton (7)
Ashgate Primary School

Laughter

Laughter is yellow like the burning sun
Laughter sounds like clowns inside you
Laughter tastes like jelly babies
Laughter smells like daisies in a field
Laughter looks like lovely flowers
Laughter reminds me of laughter at Christmas.

Lauren Jenns (8)
Ashgate Primary School

Happiness

Happiness is as yellow as the *sun*
It sounds like a bird singing
It tastes like a fire burning
It smells like a barbecue burning
It looks like a daisy
It reminds me of me and my brother playing together.

Hellen Biete (8)
Ashgate Primary School

Love

Love is as red as a red, red apple
It sounds like a very happy person
It tastes like love will never end
It smells very fresh
It looks like a red heart
It reminds me of my family.

Zoe Smith (9)
Ashgate Primary School

Fun

Fun sounds like laughter
Fun tastes like sweet sweets
Fun smells fresh like fresh air
Fun looks like children playing
Fun reminds me of games
And is the colour of flowers.

Zoe Hanrahan (9)
Ashgate Primary School

Love

Love is orange like crumpled leaves in the autumn
Orange leaves, crunchy, orange, golden leaves that rustle in the wind
Love sounds like happy times with my friends
Happy times, laughing at jokes, cuddling and showing things
Love tastes like ice cream in a cone
Ice cream, yummy, creamy, soft and delicious
Love smells like pink roses blowing in the wind
Roses, pink, reds of all kinds, smelling as sweet as a
                                       summer's morning
Love looks like a garden full of flowers
Flowers, they smell as sweet as a summer's breeze
Love reminds me of times with my family
Families, people who are very kind and loving.

Samantha Whitby (8)
Ashgate Primary School

Transport

I can see the traffic lining up in lines
I can see the aeroplanes way up above
I can see people who are learning to drive
I can see myself in the window, who's been travelling all day.

I can hear the trains picking up the passengers
I can hear the tired taxis beeping all the way!
I can hear the lorries' music through the open window.

My mum feels the steering wheel as she leads the way
I can't really feel anything except my magazine!
All at once I look, we're there, but now I'm getting tired
I'd better get to sleep, ready for my next long journey - tomorrow!

Stephanie Brown (9)
Ashgate Primary School

Happiness

Happiness is as bright as the fresh sun shining in the fresh air
Happiness sounds like little children laughing with joy
Happiness tastes like the fresh air shining down on me
Happiness smells like beautiful roses that are glowing in the sun
Happiness looks like little children playing in the happy village,
nice and happy
Happiness reminds me of everyone playing happily in the sunshine.

Demi Hughes (7)
Ashgate Primary School

Love

Love is red like a pure red love heart
Love is pure red
Love sounds like birds singing very sweetly
Love tastes like sweet chocolate cake
Love smells like a fresh bottle of water
Love looks like someone wants to kiss you
Love reminds me of cuddling my family.

Kathleen Harty (8)
Ashgate Primary School

Love

Love is as red as a rose
Love sounds like the twang of Cupid's bow
Love tastes like cherryade lipstick
Love smells like chocolates
Love looks like Cupid's coming down from Heaven
Love reminds me of my family.

Nico Begni (8)
Ashgate Primary School

The Iron Man

I can see junk all around me
I can see bright piping
I can see sharp edges
I can see white baths everywhere
I can see coloured cars everywhere
I can see bicycles everywhere
I can see springs everywhere
I can see lorries bringing old cars in.

I can feel tingling under my feet
I can feel people collecting scrap from near me
I can feel scrap falling everywhere
I can feel heavy scrap around me
I can feel black smoke coming to me
I can feel cold metal on my hands
I can feel opaque metal shattering
I can feel heaps and heaps of metal.

I can hear people dealing good scrap
I can hear cranes clanking metal
I can hear car parts being taken out of cars
I can hear fast engines revving
I can hear spanners clanking
I can hear cars being weighed for money
I can hear car keys being thrown around
I can hear people shouting at each other.

Ryan Lambert (8)
Ashgate Primary School

Terror

Terror is the colour black
It sounds like the smashing of a car
It tastes like iron
It looks disgusting
Terror has the stench of blood.

Callum Redfern (8)
Ashgate Primary School

Soldiers

I can see explosions and fire burning down the city
Soldiers are marching around on foot
I can see people running from the fire.

I can feel fear inside me and sadness all around
I can feel the pain in my hurting foot.

I can hear bombs and people screaming loudly
Guns are going *bang, bang, bang* around me
I can hear the rain pouring loudly outside.

Kayleigh Fletcher (9)
Ashgate Primary School

Love

Love is as red as blood
Love tastes as sweet as popcorn
Love is as squeaky as a door
Love is as fresh as a bottle of water
Love looks like a bunch of roses
Love reminds me of people.

Joab Coulson (7)
Ashgate Primary School

Soldiers

I can see the soldiers getting ready to shoot
I can see the war planes above my head
And the fire burning on ahead.

I can feel the sweat pouring down my face
I can feel the sadness inside my body
I can feel the pain in my throbbing feet.

I can hear the noise of the planes flying
I can hear the bombs exploding
I can hear the yell of the people dying.

Sophie Harrison (9)
Ashgate Primary School

Happiness

Happiness is as yellow as the bright sun
Happiness sounds like a fresh apple
Happiness tastes like bright daffodils
Happiness is flowers
Happiness looks like fresh cream cakes
Happiness reminds me of yellow flowers.

Liam Heldreich (8)
Ashgate Primary School

Hate

Hate is as black as the night sky
It tastes like a burning-hot chilli on my tongue
It sounds like the roar of a lion
Hate smells like a burp
It looks like dirt
Hate reminds me of a lion's face.

Mitchell Atterbury (8)
Ashgate Primary School

Soldiers

I can see the soldiers gathering together in a circle
I can see the people shooting at other people and the buildings falling.
I can feel sweat dripping down me
I can feel the sticky mud when I walk and the pain of my hand.
I can hear the planes over me
I can hear the shouting of people dying and the sound of
                                        guns shooting.

Bethany Lawrence (9)
Ashgate Primary School

Happiness

Happiness is yellow like sunshine over me
Happiness smells like flowers in the window
Happiness sounds like trees rustling in the breeze
Happiness feels like snowflakes over my head
Happiness looks like birds flying in the sky
Happiness tastes like a spoon of sugar
Happiness reminds me of a big tin of chocolates.

Annie Horsley (8)
Asterdale Primary School

Sadness

Sadness is blue like water
Sadness sounds like crying
Sadness tastes like bitter lemons
Sadness smells like burning
Sadness looks like creatures in the grass
Sadness feels like a spiky nail and it makes me feel lonely
Sadness reminds me of when my grandad died.

Megan Cartwright (8)
Asterdale Primary School

Love

Love is red like a love heart
It sounds like a beating heart
It smells like a bunch of roses
It looks like a dolphin jumping through the sea
It tastes like kisses
Love reminds me of a shooting star
Love feels like a butterfly.

Hollie Miller (8)
Asterdale Primary School

Anger

Anger is red like a fierce fire with red flames
Anger sounds like an exploding bomb
Anger tastes sour like a big, juicy lemon
Anger smells like a boiling pot of water
Anger looks like a charging bull with big, pointed horns
Anger feels like a hot, boiling volcano with big splashes of orange lava
Anger reminds you of a rumbling car engine.

Joe Cokayne (8)
Asterdale Primary School

Anger

Anger is red like an exploding bomb
Anger smells like burning hot fire
Anger reminds you of a charging bull
Anger tastes like bubbly hot water
It feels like a volcano with lava running down it
Anger sounds like yelling and shouting
Like a monster with threatening claws.

Tamara Thompson (8)
Asterdale Primary School

Jealousy

Jealousy looks like people being horrid
Jealousy feels like shouting down your ear
Jealousy tastes like rotten apples
Jealousy smells like meat
Jealousy sounds like shouting.

Katrina Thompson (8)
Asterdale Primary School

Fear

Fear looks like a scary dream
Fear feels like a rusty knife
Fear tastes like rotten pears
Fear smells like rats in mud
Fear sounds like someone crying.

Kieran Eames (9)
Asterdale Primary School

Fear

Fear looks like a fire
Fear feels like a frosty hand grabbing my arm
Fear tastes like glass going down your throat
Fear smells like blue cheese
Fear sounds like someone scraping their fingernails
                                      down the blackboard.

Ben Cooper (8)
Asterdale Primary School

Love

Love looks like a burning, red-hot fire
Love feels like really soft teddies
Love smells like roses
Love tastes like treacle with custard
Love sounds like my mum's voice.

George Lawrenson (9)
Asterdale Primary School

Hate

Hate looks like greedy people
Hate feels like someone pushing me over
Hate smells like horrible things
Hate tastes like gone off fruit
Hate sounds like someone falling over on the playground.

Thomas Erskine (8)
Asterdale Primary School

Envy

Envy is dark black
Envy smells like rotten eggs
Envy tastes like mouldy oranges
Envy sounds like people shouting
Envy is like a hard wall.

Zak Merrin (8)
Asterdale Primary School

Love

Love is people loving their friends and mums and dads
Love smells like flowers in a field of fresh grass
Love feels like chocolate fudge cake
And hot chocolate going down your throat
Love sounds like birds singing.

Jemma Hawksworth (8)
Asterdale Primary School

Hate

Hate looks like a rough and hard rock
Hate feels all sharp and bumpy
Hate smells like someone crying
Hate tastes like rotten cold grapes
Hate sounds like someone hurt.

David Oakley (9)
Asterdale Primary School

Love

Love is red and snuggled
Love is warm and fluffy
Love smells like perfume
Love tastes like hot chocolate
Love sounds like a football crowd.

Lewis Dickens (9)
Asterdale Primary School

Joy

Joy looks like a child skipping and giggling
Joy feels soft, furry and cuddly
Joy tastes sweet, soft and pure
Joy smells like sweet red roses
Joy sounds like people getting married.

Elle Ford (9)
Asterdale Primary School

Love

Love looks like a hot fire
Love smells like perfume
Love tastes like a Milky Way running down my throat
Love sounds like a steam engine
Love feels like a heart beating.

Kane Jordan (9)
Asterdale Primary School

Hate

Hate looks old and grey, like something is broken
Hate feels rotten, hard like it has been there for ages
Hate smells like an old, foul smell
Hate tastes bitter, like it's old
Hate sounds like you've broken someone's heart and hurt
                                                them so much.

Jyoti Nazran (8)
Asterdale Primary School

Fear

Fear is red like sunburn
Fear sounds like danger running through your skin
Fear feels like horror in your eyes
Fear smells like terror from your enemy
Fear tastes like the most horrible thing you've ever had to eat
Fear looks like tears running down your face
Fear is like looking at a spider when you don't like them.

Siobhan Sutton (9)
Asterdale Primary School

Love

Love is the colour of a rose
Love sounds like a fluttering butterfly
Love tastes like chocolate truffles
Love smells like an apple smoothie
Love looks like a kitten
Love feels snuggly
Love reminds me of my birthday.

Aimee Miller (9)
Asterdale Primary School

Envy

Envy is black like an endless pit
Envy sounds like old machinery screeching and squealing
Envy tastes like sick being poured down your throat
Envy smells like a room full of mouldy vegetables
Envy looks like a big, black, spiky blob
Envy feels like needles pricked into your skin
Envy reminds me of evil thoughts creeping into people's minds.

Jessica Woods (10)
Asterdale Primary School

Happiness

Happiness is laughter filling the air
Happiness is the colour of a rainbow
Happiness tastes like bright coloured sweets
Happiness is like a lovely smile
Happiness is something exciting going to happen
Happiness reminds me of you.

Lauren Secker (9)
Asterdale Primary School

Anger

Anger is red
Anger is bad
No one likes it
Because it goes through your head.

Anger sounds like screaming
It sounds like Hell
It sounds really bad
That's the reason people get unwell.

Anger tastes like blood out of an opened wound
It tastes like mud off the dirty ground.

Anger smells like fresh guts of an animal's body
And smells like rotten bodies rotting on the ground.

Anger looks like the Devil's face staring you in the eyes
It looks like a hand hitting someone in the face.

It feels like a knife stabbing your heart
It feels like a fist punching your nose.

It reminds me of a fight between my sister and this girl
They were fighting in the street getting me really angry and mad.

Carly Bates (9)
Asterdale Primary School

Sadness

Sadness is the colour of black
Sadness sounds like thunder
Sadness tastes like a cold ice cube melting on your tongue
Sadness smells like a rainy day
Sadness looks like a dirty puddle lying there on the ground
Sadness feels like you're all alone and you have nothing
Sadness reminds me of my pet dying.

Becky Painter (10)
Asterdale Primary School

Love

Love is a nice cup of hot chocolate
Love is like a nice fluffy carpet
Love is a warm fire
Love is a big cuddle at bedtime
Love looks like a cuddly bear
Love feels like a nice thing
Love reminds me of happiness.

Ryan Mason (9)
Asterdale Primary School

Love

Love is the colour of a red love heart
Love sounds like beautiful happiness
Love tastes like happiness when you wake up
Love smells like wonderful signs
Love looks like happy people smiling
Love feels like a good sign
Love reminds me of birds tweeting.

Rebecca Stainforth (9)
Asterdale Primary School

Love

Love is the colour red
Love sounds like babies laughing
Love smells like perfume
Love looks like teddy bears singing
Love tastes like a sweet
Love reminds me that it is so sweet
Love feels like a creamy chocolate.

Nyasha Chabaya (9)
Asterdale Primary School

Emotion Poem

Love is the colour of red cherries
Love sounds like people having fun
Love tastes like a red apple
Love smells like happiness
Love looks like a cute teddy bear
Love feels like a soft, fluffy pillow
Love reminds me of the colour red
It reminds me of keeping a family together.

Anger is the colour red
Anger sounds like someone shouting
Anger tastes like blood
Anger smells like people being nasty
Anger looks like an exploding volcano
Anger looks like red faces
Anger feels like the burning sun
Anger reminds me of people getting mad and shouting.

Hate is the colour blue
Hate tastes like people being nasty
Hate smells like people being nasty and fighting
Hate looks like people having a go at each other
Hate feels like a brick wall
Hate reminds me of people falling out.

Gemma Jackson (10)
Asterdale Primary School

Happiness

Happiness is red like a rose
Happiness sounds like birds singing
Happiness tastes like ice cream
Happiness smells like a rose
Happiness looks nice and fluffy
Happiness feels like a plump pillow
Happiness reminds of the six weeks holiday.

Stuart Morris (9)
Asterdale Primary School

Love

Love is pure red like a blooming rose
Love sounds like the heart of someone running in the wind
Love tastes like juicy, ripe strawberries on a sunny day
Love smells like lovely sweet perfume
Love looks as beautiful as a giant waterfall
Love feels wonderfully sweet
Love reminds me of Romeo and Juliet.

Annie Sheldon (9)
Asterdale Primary School

Love

Love is red like a heart pumping
Love sounds like fireworks
Love tastes like champagne
Love smells like perfume
Love looks like peace
Love feels like Heaven
Love reminds me of my sweetheart.

Laura Colder (9)
Asterdale Primary School

Love

Love is the colour of a red-hot, fierce dragon
Love is the sound of a romantic night in
Love is the taste of melting chocolate
Love has the smell of a hot roasting dinner
Love has the look of nice, juicy strawberries
Love feels like love hearts
Love reminds me of Valentine's Day.

Jade Cousins (10)
Asterdale Primary School

Love

Love is red like a bright poppy
Love sounds like soft crashing waves
Love tastes like a juicy red apple
Love smells like bright, happy flowers in the sun
Love you can't see, but you know love is there
Love feels like colourful butterflies flying around your heart
Love reminds me of a bunch of red, soft flowers.

Thomas Cox (10)
Asterdale Primary School

Love

Love is red like the warmth of the sun
Love sounds like your heart beating, *boom, boom*
Love tastes like strawberries, juicy and sweet
Love smells like roses glowing red
You cannot see love, but it's always in your heart
Love makes you tingly inside
Love reminds me of a beautiful sunset over the horizon.

Emily Tomlinson (10)
Asterdale Primary School

Love

Love is the colour of a red heart
Love sounds like happiness in the air
Love tastes like having a cup of cocoa
Love looks like a sunny day
Love smells like a strong rose
Love makes you feel happy and cheerful
Love reminds you of angels in the warm air.

Daniel Page (10)
Asterdale Primary School

Happiness

Happiness is the colour yellow
Happiness is joyful and sounds like people laughing
Happiness tastes like sweet strawberries
Happiness looks like people smiling
Happiness feels like joy is exploding inside you
Happiness reminds me of when my family get together.

Lauren Spencer (9)
Asterdale Primary School

Fear

The colour of fear is yellow like yellow bellies
The sound of fear is teeth chattering
The taste of fear is sick
The smell of fear is sweat
The look of fear is pale skin
The feel of fear is trembling
What reminds me of fear is spiders.

Sam Wilson (10)
Asterdale Primary School

Happiness

Happiness is a shiny rainbow colour
Happiness sounds like a long-lasting bell
Happiness smells of clear, fresh air
Happiness tastes so nice and sweet
Happiness looks wonderful and smily
Happiness feels like you want to run free
Happiness is a clear blue sky.

Hayley Binfield (9)
Asterdale Primary School

Love

Love is the colour of red strawberries
Love sounds like my mum's heart beating
Love tastes like hot dinners
Love looks like the moon in the night
Love feels like hot milk
Love reminds me of my cat.

Jason Carpenter (9)
Asterdale Primary School

Love

Love is the colour of a bright, shining heart
Love is a warm welcoming smile
Love tastes like a hot cup of tea
Love smells like a cup of mulled wine
Love looks like a snuggly bed
Love feels like a fluffy pillow wrapped around you
Love reminds me of happiness.

Lauren Cook (10)
Asterdale Primary School

Fear

Fear is like a black eye
Fear is like a scream from a person
Fear is like a food that can hurt you
Fear is like rotten eggs
Fear is like a ghost that scares you
Fear is like a shiver tingling down your back
Fear is like a scary movie that you watch.

Ryan Sheldon (10)
Asterdale Primary School

Love

Love is red like a balloon
Love tastes like sweets
Love smells like perfume
It feels like Heaven
It makes me happy
It reminds me of sunshine.

Jack Cartwright (8)
Asterdale Primary School

Love

Love is red like a blazing hot fire
Love sounds like angels swooping through the air
Love tastes like a pizza with everything on it
Love smells like pineapple
Love looks like a rampaging heart
Love feels like a cup of cocoa
Love reminds me of birds tweeting.

Ryan Bailey (9)
Asterdale Primary School

Football

The soaking rain pours in buckets on the saturated pitch
As the frustrated footballers crash their studs on the ground like
                                                  horses hooves
The fans cheering, chanting for their team
The men are muddy as a marsh and as sodden as rain
They battle it out for the trophy, shining silver in the dim light.

Alex Monro-Jones (9)
Bradley CE Primary School

The City
(Inspired by Gareth Owen)

When you're out in the city
Shuffling down the street
A bouncy city rhythm
Starts to boogie in your feet
The spinning London Eye
Reaches high up in the air
The evil raging wind
Messes up my curly hair
Double decker buses
Whizzing through the town
'Look, there's the Queen,
She is wearing a crown.'
Trains are swooshing by
Flying into the station
If one hits me
I'll need medication
Chemists full of poorly pills
Serving the ill
Will they get better?
I think they will
Car parks are so full
There are people in the pub
I am getting rather hungry
I think it's time for some grub.

Maisie Forton (11)
Bradley CE Primary School

My Mum

My mum is busy tidying up the mess
Complaining loudly, speeding around
Putting things in their right places
As the dog brings in dirt on his paws
My sister's upstairs throwing books onto the floor
Sorting clothes wildly.

Daniel Yeomans (9)
Bradley CE Primary School

Christmas Lunch

I can hear the sound of the pop of the fizzy champagne bottle
The giggle of all the posh dinner guests
The smash of a knocked-over glass of wine on the table
The crunch of my mother eating a hazelnut whirl
The hum of my father in the kitchen cooking shepherd's pie
The thud of my sister falling off her chair with laughter
The rustle of Celebration chocolate wrappers go round in my head
All goes quiet, all I can hear is a pin dropped on the floor
My father comes out with a massive Christmas pudding.

Rebecca Woodward (10)
Bradley CE Primary School

Pumpkin

As green as a large apple
As hard as split wood
As spotty as a tiny dog
As smooth as a baby's skin
As cold as snow
As dirty as a pig in mud
As fat as an elephant and as strong
The pumpkin is like a steady shining trophy.

Amy Mason (9)
Bradley CE Primary School

Pumpkin

As spotty as a Dalmatian dog
As fat as an elephant
As yellow as a bright sunflower
As green as a soggy apple
As a stripy as a fine zebra
As smooth as baby's skin
As dry as a hard stone.

Samantha Bebbington (9)
Bradley CE Primary School

The Warrior

Shiny silver
Jet-black
As he lifts the thrashing sword
His polished armour smashes when he walks
His shield glowing gold in the darkening light
The clatter of his axe gripped in his iron glove
His body firm and angry
His helmet secure as he leaves for battle.

Scott Galvin (11)
Bradley CE Primary School

The Cross-Country Run

The cross-country run
You get filthier and filthier
Sprinting, jogging like a motorbike whizzing on a motorway
Like a speedboat speeding on the ocean
It makes me feel tired, like I'm just going to bed
The cross-country run
Mud splurting up your back after slipping over.

Rian Galvin (8)
Bradley CE Primary School

Chris

I am sometimes black and sometimes blue
I am stormy December
I am trampled snow
I am pouring rain
I am a beautiful woolly jacket
And wellies with two pairs of socks
I am a rusty gate
I am an uncooked chicken on 'Ready Steady Cook'.

Chris Bellamy (9)
Bradley CE Primary School

Fairies

Full moon
Fairy ring
Feet dance
Mouths sing
Owls hoot
Magic hour
And an enchanted flower
Tiny wings
Buzz, flap
Huge smiles
Tree sap
Chariot
Fairy queen
More beautiful
Than ever seen
Sparkling fairies
Such a sight
Fade away into the night.

Laurel Stone (8)
Bradley CE Primary School

Winter

I opened my eyes
She had come
A crystal clear sheet of white snow
Spread across the land.
The puffs of snowflakes sprinkled still
Snowmen in every garden
Standing tall and proud.
Laughing of children
Skating on ponds
The stone houses
A snake of smoke slithers out of chimney tops
Paths of footprints beckoning me to the icy street
Trees shake off snow, coating the ground once again.

Rachel Relihan (10)
Bradley CE Primary School

The Sun

It's like a criminal of laziness
Forcing everyone to fall asleep in their deckchairs for hours upon end
Its flames lurch onto the sweaty world, unlovingly
Catching them in a trap of scorching heat
It's a bloodsucking snake, a fiery orange jewel
It's like a monstrous demon of unbearable heat, driving people mad!
It's like a security camera scanning over the planet
Everybody loves the sun, but hates it too.

Chloe Bellamy (11)
Bradley CE Primary School

The Sunflower

Hello, my sunflower
How brightly coloured you are
You're getting old mighty one
You're showing wrinkles and shivering so clearly
But how delicate you are
Fragile leaves, soft petals, yet strong stem
Now, now, don't be scared, you're lonely, I know
Come on, share your secrets with me.

Natalie Campbell-Lyons (10)
Bradley CE Primary School

The Cycle Race

I watched as they zoomed past
Their wheels spinning as fast as twisters
One most important to us
126
Cheering as they went past
Clapping
The race passed
We could only see outlines and shadows
Down the long, winding road.

Sam Bigland (10)
Bradley CE Primary School

My Sporty Friend

Built like a lion, fast, keen, cunning
Like a cheetah running for his prey
Like a football player zooming for the ball
He makes me feel slow like a snail
Like he doesn't even notice me
My sporty friend reminds me to run.

Thomas Weston (8)
Bradley CE Primary School

The Sea

The sea,
Deep, dark, slashing
The waves go wild
Crashing and turning
The waves leap like striking panthers
The sea churns like a bubbling cauldron
It makes me feel intimidated
I feel as if I am wrapped in a cage
A cage of the ocean and can't get out
It is the sea
It holds deep secrets.

Maria Webb (8)
Bradley CE Primary School

Fireworks Night

Rockets zoom through the air
Making sparkling lights
When you see a Catherine wheel
It sparkles like a night sky bright
A sparkler is fun, a sparkler is hot
When you see a sparkler
It lights up like a dot
It sizzles like a star.

Nicola Hartley (7)
Brassington Primary School

My Zoo

At my house I have a zoo
With creatures all shapes and sizes
When I take them to the show
I come out with 50 prizes!

I have a mouse the size of a house
A rat as cute as a cat
A dog as visible as fog
And I'm very proud of that.

At my house I have a zoo
With creatures big and small
I have so many in the house
I have to use the school!

I have a parrot with a beak like a carrot
A snake as fat as cake
A tiger as tall as the Eiger
And they all swim in the lake.

But of all those animals strong and weak
The worst would definitely be
Someone who likes bossing me around
My mum it has to be!

Josephine Gilbert (10)
Brassington Primary School

I've Got . . .

I've got a puppy and it is very fluffy
I've got a dog and its fur is like fog
I've got a phone and it's very well known
I've got a mum and she makes my life fun
I've got a duck and it doesn't mind my pup
I've got a mate who likes to skate
I've got a pig that likes to dig
I've got a dad and he is very mad
I've got a friend who likes to bend
What have you got?

Owen Wilkinson (10)
Brassington Primary School

There Once Was A Rat

There once was a rat,
Who was chased by a cat.
He ran into a hole,
But there a mouse had a pole
And hit him on the head
So the rat went to bed.
But then the rat had to go
For he'd lost his toe.
He went on a Jeep
Where he found a sheep.
He asked about his toe
But the sheep said, 'No!'
But also the sheep said,
'You might try the cow
Who lives with the sow.'
So he went to the cow
And the cow said, 'Ow!'
If you thought that was true
Then a fool are you!

Thomas Ball (9)
Brassington Primary School

Skies

There are lots of different kinds of skies
There's red ones, blue ones, grey ones and white ones.
And there's day ones, night ones, morning ones and evening ones.
How many skies are there?
There are 1, 2, 3, 4, 5 and more and more and more.
My dog jumps up to try and catch stars and the moon and even the clouds, so does my cat.
I have lots of pets
Yes I do
And they all try to catch the stars
Yes they do.

Chenma Hayhurst (8)
Brassington Primary School

Creatures That Lie In The Zoo

In his cage lies a chimpanzee
He's being stung on the nose by a bumblebee,
Along the path in an underwater lair
Lives a crocodile waiting there.

Around the corner a lion waits
A visit from you he really hates
A snake coils around a tree
He slithers around his cage with glee.
A tiger breaks out of the zoo
She's around the corner waiting for you
Here's a giraffe with a neck so long
She bites off branches with her rough tongue
But don't forget the most dangerous animal in the zoo is
You!

Grace Charlton (10)
Brassington Primary School

My Animals

My dog is as long as a log
My cat is as small as a rat
My parrot is the colour of a carrot
But my hippo is better than that!

My fish is as hard as a dish
My toad is as flat as a road
My snake is as still as a rake
But my hippo is more of a load!

My hippo eats lemon and curd
But is still as light as a bird
He sucks his thumb with mustard
But died cos he was absurd!

Daisy Howstan (9)
Brassington Primary School

Season

Spring
The grass starts to grow bright and green
The flowers start to blossom and smell all day long
The colourful butterflies flutter in the spring.

Summer
At last it's summer
Time to have a longer day
Flowers smell extremely nice
The hotter it becomes
The longer we can sunbathe.

Autumn
The leaves start to fall to the ground
As beautiful as ever
The birds are not singing
Because they're getting ready to hibernate
Does that mean winter's coming?

Winter
It's winter at last
It starts to snow
Never know what, it could even cover the world
Seeing the snow
Being thrown
Woolly hats being worn.

Annabel Yau (10)
Granby Junior School

Flowers

Flowers come in all different colours
Red, pink, yellow and blue
There are small ones and big ones
Some old and some new
They all have their own shape
But I think they smell great!

Chloe Timmis (10)
Granby Junior School

Tigers

Tigers walk
Can they talk?
Tigers run
Away from the gun
Their stripes shine
Mostly the orange line
They crawl through the bush
The hunters shout, 'Shush!'
Tigers stay still
When they're away from Bill
Bill shouts to Lil, his wife,
'Let's ruin this tiger's life!'
All of the tigers hear them say that
But they have got the biggest cat!
The tiger cat comes out
And frightens the horrid hunters away!
The cubs lie on the hay
With the rest of the tigers
And from now on nobody will come
To the tiger's den.

Anya Holland (9)
Granby Junior School

Hallowe'en

H ocus pocus
A ll the witches gather
L ong crooked noses
L azy fat cats
O ver the moon they fly
W itches cackling in the sky
E veryone beware
E veryone watch out on Hallowe'en
N ight!

Laurie Plant (9)
Granby Junior School

My Dog Scruff

Woof, woof, scruffy dog
What have you done?
Chased the cat
And had such, such fun.

Woof, woof, scruffy dog
What have you done?
Chased a stick, big and thick
In the hazy sun.

Woof, woof, scruffy dog
What have you done?
Sniffed around like a hound
Looking for a tasty bun.

Woof, woof, scruffy dog
Now what have you done?
I'm asleep in my bed
That's what I have done.

Lucy Detheridge (10)
Granby Junior School

Tribute To My Pet Rat

I miss my pet rat
He was so fat
He stuffed all his food
Till he could not move
He was always friendly
Never scary
However my friends
Were always wary
They never liked his big long tail
It used to make them scream and wail
But I don't care about the rest
To me he was always the best!

Abigail Sisson (10)
Granby Junior School

My Ball

I like my ball
Because it is so very small
But once it went over the wall.

I like my ball
When my friends come to call.

I like my ball
Because it is so very small
But once it went over the wall.

I like my ball
Because when it bounces, it bounces so tall.

I like my ball
Because it is so very small
But once it went over the wall.

I like my ball
And that's about all for my ball
Because it went over the wall!

Sophie Barratt (9)
Granby Junior School

It's Not Just Me!

I see something moving, what can it be?
Is it a ghost, or is it just me?
I see a shadow, what can it be?
Is it a ghost, or is it just me?
I hear a whispering, what can it be?
Is it a ghost, or is it just me?
I see a light, what can it be?
Is it a ghost, or is it just me?
It's in my room, what can it be?
It's a ghost, so it's not just me!

Carly Baker (10)
Granby Junior School

I Want To See The World

I want to see the ocean deep
I want to peep
Peep into the jungle
I want to be just like you, an explorer because
You get to see all you want to
I want to see the sun up close, so bright
Twinkling in my eyes so light
I want to see a rainbow and go to
The end where the gold will slowly flow
I want to see the snow in heaps
I want to see frogs all leap
I want to see all the ancient parts
I want to ride on old wagon carts
I want to see the world!

Georgina Thornley (10)
Granby Junior School

A Storm Beast

A storm is like a beast,
The wind howls and growls,
The rain drips and drops,
The thunder crashes and flashes,
The storm's telling you it's a beast.
It makes you panic, it makes your heart thump.
It feels mysterious and makes you frightened,
It's like a beast that's caught its prey.
It stops bashing and flashing and crashing,
You go outside to face your fear,
Until you find it's totally clear.
    But!
No, it's the beast, it's still howling and growling,
It's jumping and thumping,
Around in misty air.

Jade Chan (9)
Hilton Primary School

The Storm Creatures

The storm is a creature
High up in the sky.
It creeps past your window
Like an eagle in the air.

It comes quietly as a mouse,
At first it is silent
But then it awakens
And howls its first morning roar.

The thunder's ear-piercing,
As it crashes around.
As lightning wakes up,
And flashes throughout the evening sky.

The rain is torrential,
Like a monster pouring water
From giant monster buckets
All over the world.

Jemma Webster (9)
Hilton Primary School

Thunder And Lightning

Thunder is loud
You can hear it anywhere
It is an elephant walking
He rattles the ground with the noise.

Lightning is scary
It is like a fire burning
Lightning causes a bang
It can destroy towns and cities.

Thomas Reardon (10)
Hilton Primary School

The Snow

The snow is a big white fluff ball
That sounds like the tiniest pat.
When you step on it, it crunches and melts
And covers you toe to hat!

It feels so fresh and frosty,
You shiver when it falls on your face.
When it settles on your hands,
It slushes and what's left? Not one trace.

It sprinkles down as snowflakes,
It looks like tiny white stars,
When it falls on your face
You go freezing and your face goes hard.

Josie McCormick (10)
Hilton Primary School

The Wind

The wind is like an enemy from above,
Brushing aside everything in its path.
The wind is a wild animal,
It can harm anything in its wake.
The wind is loud, vivid or maybe violent,
But it can just be a gentle breeze.
It does not care for anything or anybody at full speed,
But it still can be violent at very short notice.
At night, when people sleep, it causes havoc,
Rustling leaves and blowing the trees around like hay.
It creeps quietly through open doors,
Waking people who need to sleep.

William Hardie (9)
Hilton Primary School

The Wind

The wind makes howling sounds,
he swivels round and round.
Then he slowly settles down
and moves on to a different town.

He is a ginormous dragon breathing fire,
as he gets higher and higher.
The wind blusters down the streets
and travels round and round your feet.

Alice Francis (10)
Hilton Primary School

Hail

Hail is an ice arrow that comes down from the sky
The archer throws them down and makes them fly.

The clatter and the screams are all you can hear,
Children all run inside like it is their greatest fear.

The arrows are painful and sting,
They get thrown down with a mighty fling.

Hail rarely comes, only when it's cold
And when it's gone, it's like a story never told.

Dan Hicklin (10)
Hilton Primary School

Storm

A storm is an army coming to rule the town,
You can hear the marching of their feet throughout the land,
They shoot down flashes of light to cut out all the power,
They throw down ice arrows that are fierce,
They throw down water to make us scared,
But gradually they give up and go away,
Then all is quiet.

Megan Russell (10)
Hilton Primary School

The Big Storm

The thunder is a giant, crashing through the earth,
He stamps through, pouring rain on anything in sight.

The wind howls strong,
Pulling at the trees,
Trying to knock us off our feet.

The rain batters down,
Knocking at the windowpanes.

Leaves rustle, people in a hustle,
All trying to get home.

Crash, smash, bang, clang,
All these noises can be heard.

A mysterious sky leaves the world in darkness.

The bangs, like saucepans, suddenly get louder,
And the rain saturates more than ever.

But finally, like magic,
The rain stops,
Crashes are silenced,
Wind dies down,
Now the ground is dry.

Alex Millington (10)
Hilton Primary School

The Wind

The wind whistles,
The wind blows,
It's like spirits' heads blowing along.

The wind knocks things over,
I'm feeling quite scared
As it rustles leaves over and down the street stairs.

The wind rumbles like a hungry bear's tummy,
It screeches and howls,
It feels quite funny.

Charlotte Harlow (9)
Hilton Primary School

Storm

The wind is a wolf getting at the doors,
It's getting at the windows with its paws.

The rain is a pain
Going down the drain.

They join together to make a storm,
Now another one is born.

The storm feels like ice,
So it's good we're having rice.

It's like the Arctic round here,
The rain's like arrows, not beer!

The storm's like a monster in the air,
Now it's cleared up, let's launch the flare.

Thomas Brown (10)
Hilton Primary School

Thunder And Lightning

Thunder and lightning are bad,
They make a child feel sad,
They are like a whole big town
Being rattled by a giant clown.
They are so strict
That you can't predict
When things are going to come.
The lightning's shape is a zigzag,
The thunder sounds like a big bang.
Lightning strikes the people,
The thunder shakes a beetle,
Let's hope it will not come again.

Mostafa Sallam (9)
Hilton Primary School

Wind And Rain

The wind and rain
Starts again, it blows down trees,
It smashes houses
And gives you fears,
You slip and slide down the street,
And you'll be having very cold feet,
Your clothes get soggy in the rain,
Let's hope there's no rain again,
The wind is back, back to blow,
And the rain will make the rivers flow,
Everyone is under the weather,
Fingers icy cold,
The rain is like an eagle soaring through the sky.
It blew and blew and rained for days
And then one day it stopped.

George Bloor (9)
Hilton Primary School

Snow And Ice

The world has gone white,
The animals are hiding away,
Turning the dark, gloomy earth
Into a fresh, icy blanket.
The snow is a big white
Ball of cotton wool unwrapped.

The snow is like a cold white monster,
The snow is a big, big, white full moon,
I slip on the ice and everybody laughs,
The world has gone white,
The animals are hiding away.

Naomi Murfin (9)
Hilton Primary School

Storm

Rumble of thunder,
Flash of lightning.

Frightened children,
Soggy, drenched clothes.

Great downpour,
Steamy windows.

Dangerous roads,
Chilly weather like a frost demon.

Banging noises,
Roaming wind is a giant blowing.

Gushing water,
Black darkness.

Alexandra Robinson (9)
Hilton Primary School

Wind

It howls round the dark street
Biting at your hands and feet.

It whistles round trees,
It nips at your knees.

It will find a place where you're sat,
It creeps quietly like a cat.

Ready to pounce at any moment,
Better be careful of your movement.

It rattles the willows,
Children hide under their pillows.

It's a wolf howling,
It goes creeping and prowling.

Alice Genders (10)
Hilton Primary School

My Life As A Trainer

The box lid moved,
the day had come
to get all muddy.
I had been in my shoebox,
clean, with my gold still shining
and my red still colourful.

The nightmare began when
she tightened my laces,
as tight as I could take it.
I went outside in the muddy garden.
As she began to run around,
I began to get very muddy.

After she had run round many times,
it was time for me to get washed, then dried
and put into my shoebox.

Tiffany Belfield (8)
Hollinsclough CE Primary School

Pinky The Gerbil

Pinky the gerbil lies in this box
Her body still and cold,
Her grave surrounded by pretty red rocks,
Pinky was very old.

There will be no more biting of the bars,
The wheel will squeak no more,
I'll miss her eyes as red as Mars
And the tiny scratches on the floor.

Sara Bradley (9)
Hollinsclough CE Primary School

Snail

Here lies my snail
which had a silver trail,
he was one of the creatures
who loved silver features,
then he drowned
on top of a crown-shaped
bucket of silver paint.

Julie Mellor (11)
Hollinsclough CE Primary School

Georgina

Here lies Georgina the goldfish,
who, while the cat was licking her lips
for the last time, swam round her bowl.
Now she has gone up to fishy Heaven
Where she will be not a goldfish but a soul.

Joe Middleton (10)
Hollinsclough CE Primary School

My Fish

Here lies my fish who had no name,
but she was not the same as all the rest,
for she had black and white scales
and a deep orange tail
and I think she was the best,
but now she's gone I will still remember her
as the black and white fish she was.

Molly Hadfield (8)
Hollinsclough CE Primary School

In Memory Of Peter The Guinea Pig

Sprinting around the racing track,
Round there Peter dashed,
Gaining every prize he saw,
The record has been smashed.

Taking a break from all those things,
Floating to Heaven with guinea pig wings.

Buried with my grandma's seed
For worms and maggots his flesh now feeds.

I'll miss my naughty guinea pig
Brought up in a pongy pet store.

No one can replace my guinea pig
Not two, or three or more.

Ella Middleton (9)
Hollinsclough CE Primary School

Sally The Suitcase

I was born in B&Q,
I love leather polish to make me really shiny,
I hate stickers, I have had so many stickers stuck on me
that now I have a sticker phobia.

When I see other suitcases having a horrible time,
it makes me sad.
I am afraid when we visit the airport,
it just means that I'll get pushed and pulled
and dragged across the chewing-gum covered pavement,
and get thrown around.

I am relieved and happy when we arrive home,
I'm put to bed on top of the wardrobe.

Georgiana Oddy (11)
Hollinsclough CE Primary School

A Bottle Of Lucozade

I like to be left alone in the icy cold fridge with my best friends,
                                        Coke and Fanta.
We also like annoying the shopkeeper by falling out of the fridge.

But none of us like to be snatched out of the cosy fridge,
We especially don't like being sold to rotten humans.

It makes me sad when people drink my body fluids
Because it all gets wasted on a human.

It makes me afraid when someone picks me up because I know
                                        they will squeeze me
And the dreadful moment is when they drink me.

But we all like it when we are at the back of the fridge
So no one will pick us up.

Zachary Ralph Jupp (10)
Hollinsclough CE Primary School

Creamy The Guinea Pig

Here lies Creamy the guinea pig.
As good as gold she was
with long, sharp claws,
as long as dogs' paws.
Her teeth were sharp,
her fur was like sand,
but she was frightened of a human hand.
But no more scratching on the wire
and no more snores,
and a lost friend of Ginger
and no more banging the doors.

Shannon Belfield (9)
Hollinsclough CE Primary School

The Football Trainer

I am a trainer,
I liked it when I had just been bought from Allsports
and I was really clean and had no feet in me.

The nightmare began when the boy put his sweaty feet in me
and pulled my laces and strangled me.
I nearly died!

He got me and he was walking to the car,
I was nearly crying because I was getting scratched.
We got in the car, we arrived at the football stadium.

I shouted, 'No,
when is it going to be me
on the football pitch?'

The ball started towards me
and slapped me on the face.
I cried all day and I got really muddy.

I got to my new home.
He cleaned me and put me away.
I was really happy again.

Harry Johnson (11)
Hollinsclough CE Primary School

Disco Dancing

The dizzy dancing duck was dancing on the stage,
The dog was dazzled by the disco lights,
Dormouse rattled his cage,
Dragon did the barbecue with his hot breath,
Daddy-long-legs burned to death.

Georgina Ball (7)
Hollinsclough CE Primary School

Tiger

Here lies the old tiger
Under the grand oak,
With Thomas thinking it was all a joke.
Her old rubber ball rolling around,
It reminds me of when she used to bound.
Tiger was a stripy cat
She had her own special wool mat.
She will always be missed,
She never hissed,
And now she lies
Up in the skies.

Samantha Fletcher (8)
Hollinsclough CE Primary School

Rudopth The Fish

Here lies Rudopth the fish,
He was always bored with swimming and his nose was very shiny,
Now he's underground and his bones are very tiny.

Joshua Slack (10)
Hollinsclough CE Primary School

A 5 Pound Note

I liked being crisp in a big warm suitcase
until someone picked me up and
dropped me in a puddle.
Then there was a smell of leather,
the dreaded wallet.
I was crunched up for a while
then put on the radiator to dry.
Later on I was put in a wallet
then taken to a pub and
put in a till with my friends.

Jamie Beresford-Cook (11)
Hollinsclough CE Primary School

£5 Note

The till flew open,
I was ripped out
And shoved in someone's pocket.
I was just hoping that I was going back in the till,
But then I was pulled out and put on the side.
Then I was dropped in the bank with my friends.

Max Hertzog (8)
Hollinsclough CE Primary School

My Life As A Violin

I like a nice long play and a polish so I'm clean
to be played in front of an audience.
I hate it when I'm given to children who can't play
and am plucked until my strings fall off.
It makes me shriek when this happens and shake like a leaf
so now you know why I squeak.
But I love it when I'm taken for a new set of strings
and a tune that is better than ever.
So I'm played even more and I can shine in all my glory
and be loved for evermore.

Luke Keeling (10)
Hollinsclough CE Primary School

Elvis

Here lies Elvis
The king of rock and roll
I met him in the park once
And then he fell down a hole.
He ate a lot of sugar
He actually got quite fat
He had a smart white coat
And he had a tall thin hat.

Matthew Bradley (8)
Hollinsclough CE Primary School

Snow White Auditions

Tall, brown building:
Assembly rooms.
Walk in extremely nervous,
Slowly tiptoeing up the stairs.
Big crowd of people.

Into the auditioning room,
There sit the judges,
Tall and skinny,
Pointy noses,
Eyebrows raised.

Learn the dance;
Show it to the judges,
End of audition.
Legs trembling with fear,
Sweat trickling down my face.

Sent out of the room,
A while later sent in,
Judges saying,
'You sit here and you sit there.'
First side out; second side auditioning again.

Our side:
Extremely nervous,
Judges whispering,
'Are they in or out?'
'They are in Snow White at the Assembly rooms.'

Yippee! Tell my mum -
She's very proud of me.
She hugs me, she kisses me.
Then says . . .
'Oh no, more running around for me!'

Hannah Wagg (9)
Mickleover Primary School

At The Gymkhana

Sun shining upon the warm up field,
Ponies trotting around.
Children plaiting their horses up,
Waiting for their turn to ride.

I'm waiting in the warm up field
Watching the first rider coming out.
I feel my face burning
As I walk into the ring.

I canter round,
And clear the first fence
'Keep going,' shouts Mum.

I turn to the next fence,
We clear that too.
Which one's next?
Oh no, I've forgotten.

My pony runs to a fence,
She knows where to go,
She leaps over,
And she clears it.

There's one last fence,
I know which fence it is,
There's silence from the people watching,
But then a burst of screams.
We clear it.

My heart's pounding hard,
Waiting to know who's won,
And the winner is . . .
I scream with happiness,
We've won! We've won!

Lydia Roworth (9)
Mickleover Primary School

The Show

We were all there ready,
At opening night.
We were sitting there waiting,
They turned out the lights.

Suddenly it started,
With a roll of the drum
It was great fun to see
The King of Pride Rock with his son.

As the play went on
And the tension was mounting;
Suddenly he let go
And fell to the ground roaring.

After the play was over,
We went out to tea,
That was a fantastic show we saw,
Just my friend, Mum and me.

We were staying at Rebecca's,
I couldn't go to sleep;
We kept talking about the show,
Mostly the bits that made us weep.

We had great fun in London,
My favourite bit was The Lion King.
We went home the next day,
That was a great weekend.

Alex Nelson (9)
Mickleover Primary School

I Went To The Pet Shop

I went to the pet shop,
With my money;
Very much hoping to buy a bunny.

It was April 2003
We went to the pet shop
My mum, dad, brother and me.

The hamsters I bought were
Very small, I love them
They love me, but they sometimes
Drive me up the wall.

The Chinese hamsters were
Quite big, but if I bought
Them a cage all they would do was
Dig, dig, dig.

We got two hamsters
In a box
To choose these guys
It took about 15 minutes approx!

When we got into the house
I told them,
'This is what I call home,'
But of course to them,
It looked like Rome!

Keely Glynn (9)
Mickleover Primary School

Mickleover Vs Riverside

Rows and rows of emerald grass
Flowing back and forth in the wind.
Birds swooping and squawking,
Waiting for the whistle to blow.

We are fighting over the ball;
Then we had a shot,
And put it in the corner.
The crowd cheered with joy!

They came round with a goal;
We were a bit worried then . . .
A dog ran on the pitch,
Chasing it round and round and finally we got it off.

Continuing the game, the score 1-1
One of ours was fouled and then he scored.

It was their corner, 2 minutes left
It was so close; so close!
Then their player misses the goal
And then the ref blew his whistle and we won the score 2-1.

Going home with joy,
We won a football with the Derby autographs
And a celebration.

Thomas Robson (9)
Mickleover Primary School

Mid-Air Terror

'That's us,
Gate one hundred,
England we're coming home!'
I run around in circles.

Row one, two, three, four,
'I'm on the window,' I say.
We're off.
'Weeeeeeeee!'

'Mum, look,
One of the pilots is looking for cabin crew,'
Hmph; ooh,
Woh, we're falling!

The food trolley is attacking people on the plane,
Here comes the other pilot,
'Ouch!' He hits the sleeping pilot.
Hooray! We're levelling out.

Chris Mann (10)
Mickleover Primary School

Mean Mr Bowler

We go out 25 minutes to 11.00,
On each team there are seven,
Juniors vs Infants.

Goal, one, two, three!
Oh dear me, they scored three.
Ooeer! mean Mr Bowler is coming.

'Ball now!' he bellowed
Here's a problem
Middle of the game
No ball to play with

'I'll get my ball!' said James
Game continued
Oh no! They score again
Two more goals.
One minute to go;
Later, five, four, three, two, one!
Oh no! 5-0! What a scream,
We aren't a very good team!

Matthew Twigg (9)
Mickleover Primary School

The Dance Competition

Sparkling costumes hanging down,
Everyone standing nervously around,
Longing for the competition to start.

We watched all the people practising their dance,
Our mums were sticking silver stars and sequins too,
But getting glitter spray all over the place!

We had all done our dances,
Still waiting nervously to see
Whether we would win.

We waited for minutes,
Like hours it seemed,
Finally the judges came round,
Everyone stood smartly trying to impress them.

Oh no, our hearts sank down,
We had not won,
But we went home
With bronze medals around our necks!

Helen Perry (9)
Mickleover Primary School

Greek Disaster

Last summer I went to Greece.
We got on the plane;
Sat down and relaxed,
Looking forward to our holiday.

We're there; beautiful.
We see our room,
It's the biggest
In the hotel.

We unpack
And go to the pool.
It's got a jacuzzi,
Shallow end and deep end too.

At night we go out and eat,
I don't want to go,
My sister runs off,
Oh no!

We look here and there;
We can't find her anywhere!
At last we go to our room.

She's there, *phew!*

Sam Aulsebrook (10)
Mickleover Primary School

Lost Horror

Miles of rides. No end
My birthday treat had finally come.
We got a map and scored off,
We fought about which ride we went on.

Dad shouted, 'Go on the Oblivion,'
Jamie said, 'No! Go on the Black Hole!'
So we ran to the Missile.

We ran to the canteen
Dad shouted, 'Meet you at the bouncy castle!'
Jamie said, 'OK!'

Had lunch,
Nearly time to meet Dad;
But he wasn't there.

Looked in the canteen,
Looked at the Oblivion,
There was only one place to look . .

The Missile!
Ran to the queue.

Where was he?
Phew! He was at the front.

Jamie Turner (10)
Mickleover Primary School

Barking Bob

Sitting in the car,
Driving on and on,
We travel through the trees,
To pick up the small, little dog.

The dog is very jumpy,
We stroke him and stroke him,
His name is Storm,
But suddenly he runs straight through the door.

We don't like the name, Storm,
So we think of the name, Bob,
You say, 'Give your paw,'
And he's a good boy.

Wagging his tail he runs upstairs,
To see who is coming home today,
He sleeps most of the time,
But jumps up at night to come and play.

He comes to the door,
All happy and excited,
We think it's time for his walk,
So strap him up and off we go.

Across the road we walk to the fields,
We let him run around,
As he sees on the ground,
A small, yellow ball, it just fits in his mouth.

Barking at the cats,
As we run through the trees,
He chases all of the crunchy leaves,
How we love to watch his ears blow!

Georgina Barker (10)
Mickleover Primary School

Bowling Mad

I am first
Waiting to roll
Sarah, Swain, Kenzie and Libby
Are watching me.

I roll the ball
Standing watching it roll
Wondering what I'd get
Oh no, I've missed.

It's Sarah's turn
We're all watching
What will she get?
She's got two down.

Uncle Swain's turn
He's bound to win
What is it?
He got six down.

Kenzie's turn
We all cheer.
Shouting, 'Kenzie! Kenzie!'
She's got one down.

Libby's turn
We are all eager
What did she get?
She's got three down.

I've got one more go
I am nervous
What is it?
Yes, I got them all down!

Natasha Payne (10)
Mickleover Primary School

Extension, Extension

Extension, extension, you're looking so messy,
Extension, extension, this is the wrong cooker.
Extension, extension, you've got the wrong fire,
My uncle's gonna have to change them.

If the toilets are leaking
And the sinks are too.
It's not looking good
What have you done?

If there is no floor -
Where will I walk?
And I haven't got a door -
It won't be that private.

We eat somewhere else,
Round the corner we go;
We come back home
And we go to sleep.

We get up in the morning,
The toilets are still leaking.
No school!
We're happy.

My dad goes to work,
My sister's in bed,
My brother's gone berserk!
I am so mad.

Extension, extension, you've got the right cooker,
Extension, extension, you've got the right fire,
My uncle doesn't have to change it now,
Extension, extension, you're looking so tidy.

Kiran Shanker (9)
Mickleover Primary School

Florida

Boarding the plane,
After hours and hours of waiting,
Even more hours to get there,
But it's worth going.

I've been before in 2002,
Of course, it's Florida!
Where else do you think I would have gone?
Uh-oh, trouble on the plane.

My grandad has had his seat taken,
By someone from another plane,
They've gone back to their plane now,
Phew! That was a close one.

Our villa is so cool,
It's got its own swimming pool
And a Jacuzzi too.
It's not fair! My nana's got the biggest bathroom.

Yes! It's time to go to the parks,
Over the next two weeks
There's Animal Kingdom, Magic Kingdom, Epcot,
Blizzard Beach, MGM, Down-Town Disney,
Universal and Typhoon Lagoon too.

There's a massive restaurant called, Ponderosa,
It's so cool, you can eat loads,
It's nearly time to go home now!

We're going back today,
It's not fair,
Hours of waiting.
Oh no, we're back in *England!*

Emily Reader (9)
Mickleover Primary School

Legs Of Sand

What I hear, what I hear
The wonderful ocean in my ear
Children laughing,
Children playing;
Lots of children are having fun.

Mum's asleep on the sand,
Dreaming into Wonderland.
Digging holes in sand, here and there,
Make a huge hole over there
Put Matt's legs in, no over here!

He's in the hole!
Now cover him up;
Let's make some legs,
Let's pebble him up.

Placing things carefully
On the sand
It's taking shape;
It's wonderful.

One more hole, put water in it.
Just next to his feet -
'Mum, look at this!'

'Can you take a picture?'

'Okay I will.'
When *splash!*
Mum's in the hole.
What shall we do?

'I'll get you, I will.'
Mum's chasing me around.
She also gets tired and lies back down,
While I keep running round and round.

Katie Yeomans (9)
Mickleover Primary School

Football Crazy

We were on the playground,
Right next to the wall,
Waiting for Jamie,
To get his ball.

We start from the kick-off,
So very happy,
Dom does a foul,
Ryan gets snappy.

First half, nil-nil!
It's time for a break,
The teachers are having
A piece of cake!

Second half starts
On the spot,
The captains talk
About their sneaky plots.

In the second half; Tom hits the wall,
Dom hits the bin,
Olly punches the ball
And goes for a win.

They get a free kick,
Just outside the box,
Jamie so sly and cunning,
Like a nasty fox.

The ref is so strict,
But on with the game,
Dom does an own goal,
This will never be the same.

Alec James (10)
Mickleover Primary School

Rushing

My sister's tantrums wake me,
I try to stand but I'm far too weak.
I reach the door, the stairs at my feet.
I stroll downstairs like
They're never-ending - leading nowhere!

After breakfast indulgence,
I get myself dressed.
Mother screams and shouts:
We get into the car
And we're off to school.

I suddenly wake up
The panic rises inside me.
I run as fast as I can,
Taking short breaths and turning purple.
I see the school gates in the distance.

Mothers with pushchairs leaving the school grounds
I rush on.
Mr Bryan is closing the gates.
The bolts are locked. The locks locked.
I'm frantic about the telling-off I'll get.

I hesitate and approach the main entrance,
The door seems to fling open by itself.
I walk through, spots and sweat rising.
My steps feel like big leaps.
As I finally reach class 11.

Children already in position on the carpet.
I gulp! I sigh!
Slowly, I push the handle
They turn and stare at me . . .
I'm in trouble!

Alexander James Suckling (9)
Mickleover Primary School

I Got A Puppy

I got a puppy
A puppy for me
He ran away
After his tea.

I looked in the hay
Something gave a neigh!
I wondered what it might be;
Would he come today?

I rang the pound
Every day
But all they said
Was, 'Not today!'

Little did I know
The dog was fine.
And his new owner
Didn't seem to mind!

Some time later,
She walked him to the pound.

'The right owner for this dog,
Must be found!'

The man at the pound
Give me a ring,
And said to the lady,
'You've done the right thing!'

I collected the puppy,
I was as happy as could be!
I took him home,
And cuddled him on my knee.

Alice Southall (9)
Mickleover Primary School

The Match

On to the match
Went me and my dad.
Hopefully to watch
A win. Come on!

When we got there
The pitch was bare,
Then the players came rushing out
And they gave a great big shout.

People there, waiting for the whistle,
Everyone restless, off their seats.
Away fans trying to find their seats.
People singing, 'Come on you Wolves!'

At half-time I bought a treat;
I bought a hot dog to warm my feet.
Eventually they come back out
Giving an even bigger shout!

With 10 minutes to go
It was 2-2;
But with two quick goals for Wolves,
It was 4-2!

I go home and explain
All to my mum.
My dad said,
'She has to come and have some fun!'

Tom Foster (9)
Mickleover Primary School

Up Her Nose

Sitting in the living room
Playing with beads
Rebecca ran upstairs
And I heard her scream.

I start to panic,
Thinking, *what's up?*
I tremble upstairs to find . . .
'Oh no!'

I must be wrong;
It can't have happened.
I mean -
She, she, she . . .

She's got a bead stuck up her nose
'Oh no! Oh no! What can we do?'
Bring! Bring! 999
The ambulance, here it comes.

In the back of the car
We're nearly there
Puffing and panting; Achoo!

The bead shoots out!
It's all back to normal.
We turn around
And back we go.

Rhiannon Smallman (9)
Mickleover Primary School

The Crucial Match To Avoid Relegation

Crowd singing loudly,
Cheering players on.
Are we going to win?
Are we going to lose?

He runs up the football pitch;
Gets pulled down.
We are awarded a penalty,
He steps up to take it and . . .
Our heads go down.
He missed!

Moments later, we get revenge.
Ball hits the back of the net.
They go to celebrate but get too excited.
And one of our fans gets arrested.

The referee blows the half-time whistle,
We give our players a great big clap
And boo off the opposition.

They kick-off in the second half,
Twenty seconds later, we score another.

Then a drunken man runs onto the pitch
And goes to celebrate with the players.

At last the ref blows the final whistle;
'Hooray!' we cheer.
Once again we've avoided relegation;
Well, what a massive celebration.

We give the players a good old cheer
And celebrate with a bottle of champagne,
Then again we give them a clap.
We roar them off, back into the tunnel,
And leave the stadium feeling proud.

Danny Cunningham (9)
Mickleover Primary School

An Irish Dancing Competition

I'm on stage.
Everyone is staring
The music comes on
I point my toe.

I start to dance,
My right foot first.
I wobble and trip,
I hurt my foot.

I hobble off stage,
Sit on a chair.
People still dancing,
Getting medals.

I stop and stare,
Till the last dance comes.
My foot feels better
I get on the stage.

I start to dance,
Then the music stops.
I cross my fingers.
I want a medal.

The judge coughs,
Then calls out numbers.
Lucy - first
Me - second.

I collect my medal,
And hold it tight.
I thank the judges,
For such a great night.

Mollie Garratt (9)
Mickleover Primary School

Sweet Puppy Barking

Sweet puppy barking
In the pen,
Puppies running around
And around.

Picking them up and
Putting them on the grass,
Running off and hiding in the bushes
Waiting for us to find them.

Playing softly with them
And loving them to bits,
Licking me on my nose
And them playing with me too.

Putting them back in their pen
And then,
Softly,
Stroking them to sleep.

Ryan Skidmore (10)
Mickleover Primary School

Standing In The Woods In Winter

Shining ice on the ground.
Tree tops glistening with ice.
Snow falls from the sky.
Jack Frost dances in the snow,
Water turns to ice.
Silent snow falls when you're sleeping.
Jack Frost has cast a spell.
Footprints in the snow,
Show where animals have walked.

Sanchez Frank (9)
Oakthorpe Primary School

Standing In The Woods In Winter

Enchanted forest.
Sparkling snow on the trees and ground.
Robins singing their pure tunes.
The sun is gleaming,
Lighting the silvery snow.
Grey and white clouds.
Jack Frost dancing in the snow.
Snow on the treetops.
Trees shivering in the iciness.
Snow dropping from branches.
Animal footprints chase each other,
In the silvery spell.
I'm chilly.
Jack Frost will be here soon,
To sweep up the fluffy white snow.
My secret will be no more,
For my kingdom will be invaded,
By the dewdrops of spring.

Connor Cannon (9)
Oakthorpe Primary School

Standing In The Woods In Winter

Gloomy clouds overhead,
Toboggans twisting and turning.
Shiny icicles hang from branches,
They look like lightning.
Foxes in hibernation,
Trees with no branches,
All but the evergreen
Ready for snowmen to sit in a row.

David Ashworth (9)
Oakthorpe Primary School

The Winter Woods

Silent, mystical,
Glimmering snowflakes scrape my hair
Like icy fingertips.
The secret spell of snow fairies
Mystifies me.
As my feet crunch on the pure snow,
Trees majestically follow me
Like stalkers.
In the night time darkness,
I'm never alone
Dawn breaks.
Red robins swoop in the sunlight,
As snow fairies dance in the mystical light.
Jack Frost sprinkles his salt like snow,
On the high treetops of the woods.
Soon Jack Frost will be back
To sweep up his magnificent masterpiece.
Spiders cautiously decorate their webs,
With beautiful jewels,
Ready for the grand winter parade.
Snowdrops begin to fall from beyond the clouds
Soon my winter wonderland,
Will be no more.
At least I have seen my secret wood
In all its glory.
As I know it will never be the same.

Anna Southerd (10)
Oakthorpe Primary School

Standing In The Woods In Winter

Snowdrops falling on the frozen lakes,
Soft slippery topping.
Frost sitting around the sides of the lake,
Snowdrops falling on the treetops,
Feathery branches.

Callum Lennon (10)
Oakthorpe Primary School

Standing In The Woods In Winter

As winter approaches,
The sparkling snow starts to fall on us.
As the snow starts to fall
The small deep pond turns to ice,
Icicles hanging from branches of trees.
As I walk through the forest,
My feet go deep through the snow.
Jack Frost here,
Jack Frost there.
Jack Frost sprinkles his fairy dust everywhere.
I can see the decorations,
The snow has created.
As I walk through the sparkling snow,
I hear the robins sing.
I can spy cobwebs,
Glistening on the trees.
Rabbits in their burrows and badgers hibernate.
Now winter's here, shout hurrah!

Leah Commons (10)
Oakthorpe Primary School

Standing In The Woods In Winter

Standing still in the snowy woods,
Icicles hang like wizards' pointy fingers.
Footprints chase each other through a fallen fantasy.
I shiver in the iciness.
Robin redbreast's song rings out like a flute.
Naked trees cover the forest floor.
I stretch in the sunlight,
Sparkling snow crunchy where my feet are.
Sun, shivering in the sky.
My secret winter wonderland.

Olivia Bozeat (10)
Oakthorpe Primary School

The Winter Woods

Icicles hang on snowy white trees,
As they glitter in the winter forest and grow.
The sky, as white as snow.

Snowdrops land on icy lakes and melt,
Snowy trees like snowmen blow around
In the winter woods.

Robins in the woods, walking across
The white snow and rabbits
Hopping around.

Ponds and lakes frozen with ice,
Birds singing all day long.
The secret snow at night.

Kane Marriott (10)
Oakthorpe Primary School

Standing In The Woods In Winter

Bark falling from the trees,
Sparkling snowflakes above.
It feels like waking up to a new world.
You can hear howling, howling like a wolf.
Wind blowing, leaves rustling.
Conifers towering over you.
The sunlight shining down,
Casting huge shadows from gargantuan conifers.
The snow shivering down my back,
My feet crunching in the snow.
Trees look like ghostly figures,
Staring at you.
Look up into the big blue sky.

Kathryn Adams (11)
Oakthorpe Primary School

Standing In The Woods In Winter

Silent, magical, mystical, sacred.
Arctic wind blows from the north.
Falling snow from clouds
Comes to a halt.
The fresh smell of conifers and glistening barbed trees.
Tower over the horizon.
Silhouetting on the sparkling lake.
Animal den covered by snow.
Ancient tree with spiralling branches,
Bare their burden of snow.
Tall pointy trees
Peak over others,
Like tall stalagmites or mighty pillars.
The trees create pointy wizards' fingers.
A white wizard watches over us
From his cloud palace.

Jordan Barry (11)
Oakthorpe Primary School

Standing In The Woods In Winter

Shining ice on top of the treetops,
Makes the branches shiver.
Glistening snow falls from the sky.
Ice is melting,
Snow is dancing from the clouds
On to the floor.
There are footprints in the snow,
Jack Frost dances his magical dance.
Falls at night when you are sleeping.
Casts a spell on the trees.

Sabrina Collins (10)
Oakthorpe Primary School

Wish Poem

If only I could find
A dirty, smoky, diesel train that
moves as swiftly as Concorde.

If only I could find
The scariest, strongest, most skilful Pokèmon
That can crunch through rocks with its teeth.

If only I could find
A fierce and dangerous
Eagle that could take me to school everyday
On its wings.

If only I could find
The bravest warrior
Who is cunningly offering
To be my guard.

If only I could find
A gold magic, glittering coin
That is worth a brilliant £100,000
And could buy me anything I wanted!

If only I could find
A gorgeous green garden
Where a portal takes me to another world!
Where the flowers smell as beautiful
As freshly baked cakes.

If only I could find
The most beautiful mouth-watering piece of chocolate
That tickles in my tummy,
Tastebuds and toes.

If only I could find
The answers to all these wishes.
Can I? How? And what would I do if
I could find them out?

George Dixon (9)
Old Hall Junior School

Bowler's Bouncer

Clutching the new orb,
Radiant over the morning sunrise.
Focusing like a falcon approaching its prey,
Contemplating the kill.

Commencing the march
Into a stride,
Like a speeding Concorde,
The tyrannical ogre.

Landing with a clattering thump,
Onto the perfect pitch.
Releasing the orb,
Bouncing unpredictably.

The batsman
Caught unawares.
Trying to hook over the top
Caught at Deep Fine Leg.

Tom Mounsey (10)
Old Hall Junior School

The Hunter

As the evening darkness draws into the jungle,
The mighty tiger hunts his prey.
He sweeps silently through the trees,
His agile body leaps over vines
And dashes through rushing rivers.
He sprints through the whole jungle, searching.

Until suddenly, a helpless victim comes within his sights,
He crawls along the jungle soil, keeping low to the ground
Like a snake slithering across the mud.

Just then, with one thunderous pounce and a vicious roar,
The tiger silences his prey and gives it a most painful death.

Katie Swift (10)
Old Hall Junior School

Cat Fight

In the light of the moon,
The felines creep out,
Shining lenses glowing in the dark,
Razor-sharp claws trailing along the floor.

The tabby cries out loud in pain,
As the ginger punctured tabby's coat,
They look to each other
And start to gloat.

A deadly silence fills the street,
They both reach out and battle till dawn,
One last screech, like squeaky brakes,
They both join paws, 5 minutes it takes.

Then both creep away,
Until the next day.

Amy Marie Duffy (11)
Old Hall Junior School

Cats

The street was silent,
The silent street.
Two cats approaching each
Other to meet.

They stood there and stared
Into each other's eyes,
Like two schoolboys about
To fight.

Until one made a move,
They started to scrap.
Tension was building,
Then one backed down.
The other one stood
Feeling brave and proud.

Laura Harrison (11)
Old Hall Junior School

The Planets

Mercury is an ill person, always cuddling up to his blanket and his hot water bottle.

Venus is an angry person who is always hot with fury. He is always shouting at the top of his voice.

Earth is an intelligent person who is clever and has got wonderful, amazing talents.

Mars is a creative person, always building volcanoes with the red dust he can find around.

Jupiter is a nosy person, always looking at you with his stormy red eye.

Saturn is a vain person who always thinks she's beautiful, when really she's not.

Uranus is a gymnast, always doing roly-polies on his side.

Neptune is a grumpy old man always being mean and nasty and evil.

Pluto is a young child that's still at school.

Lorna Stone (10)
Old Hall Junior School

My Dog Amber

She's an electric motor, always going,
She's a pair of woolly socks on my feet most of the time,
A tiny lamb that never leaves my side.
She's got the buzz of a bee, annoying sometimes,
She's got the smell of a cosy evening in, warm and comforting.
A baby when she sleeps, soft and gentle.
She's a tissue when I cry,
She's a cheetah, as fast as light,
Basically she's an Amber,
No object could ever replace her!

Anna Stephanie Casper (9)
Old Hall Junior School

The White Waterfall

Calmness of the slow flowing water,
Moving gently along the river,
Little boats bob along the water
Like ducks swimming.

Then suddenly, your boat goes into bubbles
Like a jacuzzi, but fiercer.

There's a big loud gush of water,
Then you realise you're in white water.
It feels like you're having a heart attack,
You fear the rocks at the bottom.

As you reach the bottom, you go under,
You come back up and you're on tranquil waters,
It's like you've died and come back to life again.

Anna Elizabeth Griffiths (10)
Old Hall Junior School

The Perfect Drive!

I'm waiting for the snails in front,
Leaving an oozing trail of divots,
Clutching my grip with anticipation,
Pressing my tee in the boggy ground,
Placing the shiny new ball on the tee,
Finally, they're out of range!

Swinging round like an owl's head,
Uncoiling like a python,
Balancing as still as a hunting lion.

The ball flies through the air,
Faster than a bullet.
Soaring high into the sky,
Bounce . . . bounce . . . bounce,
Yes, yes, it's in the hole!

Ruth Rastrick (10)
Old Hall Junior School

Waterfall

Drifting silently,
Keeping the secret,
Making no noise at all,
Just a trickling sound
Running smoothly like silk.

Now rapidly changing,
Like paper being torn.
Bubbly water swishing this way and that,
Dancing water,
Falling, falling into nowhere . . .

Splash!
All is silent,
Sweet water,
Carrying on to the next adventure,
Glassy liquid, seeking rest.

Emma Dewick (11)
Old Hall Junior School

The Dragon

The ground starts to rumble,
The ground starts to shake.
Buildings start falling,
The monster is awake.

As smoke uncurls from the monster's belly,
People on the street start to run.
The monster starts roaring and shouting,
Then the creature shoots rocks out of the top
Like a loud bang from a gun.

As the dragon starts to close its eyes,
Like a baby going to sleep,
And all that's left of the town below
Is ashes deep.

Taylor Spencer (10)
Old Hall Junior School

The Hunt

Straining at the bit, steaming nostrils flaring like fire,
Pulling like a bull,
For them to let go,
The other horses are beginning,
It's time to get along!

Over the ditch, across the field,
The hounds are howling,
The sirens are starting
They found a trail!
Off we go, flying up the hill.

Here comes the Hunt,
The Hunt Master blows his horn,
'We've got him!'
A demon cornered, snapping and yowling.

Down comes the demon,
Sent by the Devil himself,
A head, a tail are all a prize.

Jade Wong (11)
Old Hall Junior School

The Storm

He started following me down the street,
I stopped, he stopped.
I started walking again, so did he
He came closer and gave me a knock.
Now he was crashing and banging me,
I tried to keep quiet but I really couldn't,
Then he gave me a powerful vicious push,
So it made me fall on my knee.
But then he made me really angry,
Blowing, twisting, fiercely,
You can't ignore a twister,
Especially one that follows you around.

Jake Armitage (9)
Old Hall Junior School

The Race

Circling the ménage not long to go,
Horses not knowing what to expect
Strangers all around,
Lights flashing everywhere.

Eventually, into the starting boxes,
Feet tingling, ready to go.
Ready to gallop off down the track,
Suddenly, click, click, starting gates open,
       Off we go!

Galloping faster, must win
Must get -
       faster
       faster
       faster must win the race
       faster
Nearly there
       faster
       faster
       Won the race!

Charlotte Eyre (11)
Old Hall Junior School

The Storm

It started at 12pm I tried to ignore it.
By breakfast it was shaking the house
By lunch it had raised Hell
By tea it had killed my pet mouse
In the evening, it had wrecked the town
Smashing through the Town Hall
People keep saying, 'God help us all!'
It won't stop for a sec
Till it leaves everything in a wreck.
You try running from a hurricane
You'll be next!

James Marriott (10)
Old Hall Junior School

The Leopard's Pounce

The gleaming eyes of the leopard
Staring, glaring,
Sparkling, shining.
Looking at the victim,
Bright in the blue moonlight.

Sneaking round to camouflage,
Sneaking with a disguise.
Crawling, creeping,
Edging towards the victim,
Slowly getting into position.

Gathering up every ounce of power,
The blood-thirsty creature,
Ferociously targeting,
Preparing for the kill,
Pouncing on the victim.

Katie Dargue (10)
Old Hall Junior School

The Feline Monster

Approaching the enemy,
The feline monster roars,
Claws rise out the tip of the paws,
Wailing, screeching, hissing
As they circle each other, round and round.

A loud screech breaks the night's silence,
The moonlight shines on the fighting felines.
Biting, scratching, bleeding,
Then silence!

Slowly the feline monsters sulk back to their territory,
Cleaning their wounds and bodies.
They fall asleep under the gaze of the moon.

Mollie Varley (11)
Old Hall Junior School

Spirit Of The Amazon

Spirit of the Amazon,
Trickling from the Andes,
Growing, growing every second.

Spirit of the Amazon,
Turning into a torrent,
A wild water rapid,
Sounding like a roaring lion!

Spirit of the Amazon,
Nearing the end of its journey,
Feeling the waves of the ocean,

Tropical fish swimming into the current,
Beginning to taste salt now,
Spirit of the Amazon.

Ruth Rastrick (10)
Old Hall Junior School

The Tranquil Lake

The tranquil lake with the still waterfall,
Calm and peaceful
Like a choir singing softly,
The sound of birds, as soothing as chime bars.
Undisturbed.

Clouds start entering the clear blue sky,
The wind starts howling like foxes in the night.
The birds dodging out of sight,
Gushing waterfall.

The rapid cheetah slowly calms down,
When butterflies glide across the stream
I gaze into the waters
As it slowly fades away.

Bethany Herrick (10)
Old Hall Junior School

The Wind

The wind walking around my house
Is a cat with sharp and shifty eyes.
Mewing and swishing its long tail.

The wind running around my house
Is a panther showing off her beautiful black coat,
Rumbling and roaring, knocking
At the windows.

The wind stalking around my house
Is a lion protecting her young,
Sneaking and growling
Waving the trees.

The wind skulking around my house
Is a jaguar glaring his teeth
Padding and drifting
Swaying the curtains.

Chloe Taylor (10)
Old Hall Junior School

The Storm

She started her silly whinge about lunchtime,
my mum said just to ignore it,
it was throwing around, banging, howling and screaming,
but I just couldn't ignore it,
by teatime it pushed down one fence,
I went to bed but all the electric had gone,
I just couldn't ignore it,
I put my pillow over my head and closed up my ears,
it was driving me up the wall,
she pushed all the bins and fences over,
I just couldn't ignore it
it got louder, it sounded like loads of babies screaming,
I was scared that the house might fall,
there were hurricanes not far away,
I just couldn't ignore it.

Peta Forder (10)
Old Hall Junior School

Fairy Tale Rap!

This is a fairy tale rap, which is gonna unfold.
You'd better listen careful cos it's going to be told.

There once was a girl called Red Riding Hood,
She lived in a cottage in a deep, dark wood.

She went to her granny's, since her granny was ill.
She didn't want to go cos she was watching 'The Bill'.

Suddenly from the bushes awoke
A friendly wolf, with a frog in his throat.

'Where are you going, my little Red?'
'I'm going to my granny's who is ill in bed.'

'Can I come with you, my little dear?'
'Course you can, it's not far from here.'

So off they went down the lane.
'I know,' said Wolf, 'we'll catch the plane.'

So off they went through the sky,
And soon enough, Granny's house was nearby.

Soon they landed in Granny's back garden,
Granny came out and said, 'I beg your pardon!'

'I'm sorry Granny, we had to catch the plane,
We would've been late and you'd have been in more pain.'

So they all went in for biscuits and tea,
And that's the end, you'll surely see.

Lorna Stone & Daisy Stopher (10)
Old Hall Junior School

The Planet From Outer Space

It's a planet we don't know much about,
It's not always Arctic cold
Sometimes it could burn you to ashes.
Really, that's all we know for now.

Ashton Hurst (9)
Old Hall Junior School

Rushing Waves

Relaxing waves,
Rippling waters,
Silent as a butterfly.

The golden ball in the sky,
Lights up the calm river.
It shines down, nothing's wrong,
Onto the calm river.

Faster and faster,
Louder and louder.
The river's getting quicker,
Rowdier and rowdier.

There is a steep drop,
Water is falling,
Falling into darkness
At the bottom, the bubble bath foams.

All is silent,
Tranquil waters seeking rest.
Water like silk,
Calm and relaxing.

Kathryn Borrell (11)
Old Hall Junior School

People Poem

If my dad was not around possibly at work full-time
I'd miss him for his funny jokes
I'd miss him for my food.
I'd miss him for his kindness and helpfulness
Round the house when he helps me tidy my room.
I'd miss his nice personality and taking me on holiday abroad
I'd miss my dad for all his good deeds such as caring for me.
So I guess my dad is someone I really need.

Laurie Woodgate (9)
Old Hall Junior School

The Storm

The light wind is a nice refreshing fan,
Cooling me on a summer's day.
Calming the Earth.

The black cloud is a grumpy old man,
Doing nothing all day.
Making the Earth sad.

The lightning is a caretaker, turning lights on and off,
Not making their mind up what they want.
Making the Earth frightened.

The rain is like a crocodile, crying its eyes out,
Never-ever stopping.
Making the Earth wet and horrible.

The thunder is a baby,
Making a real racket.
Making Earth a noisy place to be.

A hurricane is like a merry-go-round,
That goes really fast.
Making the Earth dizzy and ill.

The snow is a cold-blooded person,
Who likes to be cold and alone.
Making the Earth freeze.

The hail is like a bully,
Who likes to hurt people.
Giving the Earth wounds and bruises as it hits down.

Ellie Simpson (10)
Old Hall Junior School

The Snake

The snake glides through the desert
Like a bird through small gaps
Over sharp rocks.

Jack McKinley (9)
Old Hall Junior School

Wish Poem

If only I could find
A clumsy cat
That entertains by bumping into things.

If only I could find
A beautiful butterfly
That flies around day and night.

If only I could find
A magic mirror
That could get what I wish for.

If only I could find
A silly snake
That plays funny jokes on people.

If only I could find
A leaping lion
That leaps about in the jungle.

If only I could find
A helpful horse
That helps people that have bad problems.

Megan Biggs (8)
Old Hall Junior School

The Word Party!

Sad words are always blue,
Silly words love to mess with goo!
Fat words are always very lazy,
Happy words, people say they're crazy!
War words always ride to battle,
Sly words love to chase the cattle!
Ill words are always very sick,
Stupid words are very thick!
Gardening words need lots of hoses . . .
Snap! The dictionary closes!

Joshua Mouncer (10)
Old Hall Junior School

Cheetah Hunt

The calm wildebeest, grazing,
Zebra in the centre
As out of place as riders on the stone,
And one killer from the underworld,
An inaudible shape in the undergrowth.

Suddenly, two hungry eyes,
One thousand bloody teeth
And one terrified zebra.
The cheetah pounces, he brings down the animal,
The zebra's eyes roll,
It tries to call for help,
But the breath of life is leaving
And slowly, slowly
Its attempts cease.

The calm wildebeest, grazing,
Zebra in the centre,
As out of place as riders on the stone,
One content cheetah,
And one less animal
In a herd of one million.

David Smith (10)
Old Hall Junior School

The Storm

She started off with a strong bang,
I went away
At teatime, she was making a thundery crash
I put my earplugs in
But then, she became a roaring tornado
Banging, crashing and roaring
Don't try to ignore a storm
Not even a small one.

Ethan Alexander Iles (9)
Old Hall Junior School

A Black Silk Scarf

A black silk scarf across the sky,
With scattered pinpricks of light,
The owl lifted its head from beneath its feathers,
The night sedate, serene, tranquil.

The moon, a giant luminous ball,
The owl's silhouette passing the light,
A hunter's moon, a man may say,
As for the owl - it truly was.

Mice or rat?
Not fruit or berries
And then he spied,
A meal on the run.

As quick as a wink, knives of anger grasped,
The rodent's pulse had ceased to pound.
Ripping, shredding the skin and the flesh
From the victim's body.

Taking flight yet again,
With the sufferer in his mouth,
Into hideout where no one can see,
To enjoy his gain.

A distant light,
A far away beacon,
Came rising from the hills.

A golden gleam, a glint, a glow,
The owl's eyes slowly drooping,
And silently, gently sleeping,
As peaceful as a choir singing, softly.

Bright light gleaming,
And glory all around,
Morning had stolen the night.

Rowen Bell (10)
Old Hall Junior School

Nothing

I thought I heard
A rustle in the bushes.
'It's nothing!' I said to myself
'Nothing's there!'
I thought then I heard,
A fence creaking, creepily.
'It's nothing,' I said again,
'Nothing at all.'
But I didn't dare look in the bushes
In case I found nothing!
Standing there,
On foot or tentacle or paw.
Timidly, quiet, I kept to the track,
While nothing stalked the woods,
On great big feet.
It was strange though,
And I'd noticed this
When on my own before nothing
Was going to hurt me.

Adam Sharp (9)
Old Hall Junior School

The Storm

He always had a little strop,
But this was not the same.
He just nagged, nagged and nagged,
He made me take the blame.
When he ran viciously upstairs,
Pushing, shouting with rage,
He snapped, bashed, practically exploded
And after, he was never the same,
Just as we always expected.

Poppy Whittaker (9)
Old Hall Junior School

Black Hunters

Sleek black hunters, waiting silently,
The undisturbed battlefield is bloodless,
Sharp, fixed emerald eyes examine the opposer.

Sleek black hunters pounce;
Doggedly coming back
Scratching, biting, yelping
Then the defender flees.

Sleek black hunters,
Licking their gashes,
The black was coming
The moon was out
But the sleek black hunters
Would be back.

Ellie Burroughs (10)
Old Hall Junior School

The Silver Bolt

When the Nurbürgring's immense gates slide open,
Under the quiet village of Nurbürg,
The silver ghost slides through
Making scarcely a sound.

Over the track,
In the sturdy control tower,
The lights turn on . . . 3 . . . 2 . . . 1 . . . the lights turn off.

Like a wild beast roaring, it shoots away.
Speed unlimitless
As nimble as quicksilver,
It screams.

When the smoke clears,
The crowd's in awe,
It stands serenely,
Waiting for its next run.

Benjamin Warsop (10)
Old Hall Junior School

Wish Poem

If only I could find
the most glittering, glamorous star
that shimmered in the night sky.

If only I could find
the most cutest, cuddly kitten
that when it purred sounded like a
buzzing bee humming a tune.

If only I could find
a mysterious magic coin
that granted me any wish I wanted.

If only I could find
a magical, moving pencil
that wrote for me and did whatever I wanted.

If only I could find
a softly singing nightingale
that swooped all over the soft blue sky.

If only I could find
all of these things
then I would be the happiest
person in the world.

Amy Rees (9)
Old Hall Junior School

My Rabbit Patch

He's a ball of black and white fur rolling
around the hutch,
He's an early morning, tired, with eyes half open.
A hole in sawdust, waiting until morning to be renewed.
A comforting blanket to hug and play with,
A hungry vegetarian eating grass all day long,
He's a fragile bubble, starting a new life.

Zoë Ball (10)
Old Hall Junior School

Changing Waters

As the water trickles down the mountainside,
Over the stones and pebbles,
As calm as the night sky,
Silently flowing down, down, down.

Plucking up courage,
Changing the pace,
Listening for the sound
Of the raging waves.

Gush! Water hits water,
Massive waves
Crash up the rocks,
Of the giant cliff.

And then suddenly,
Calmness has taken over,
As still as a stone statue
A huge damp ocean.

Laura Maycock (10)
Old Hall Junior School

Wish Poem

If only I could find
A speedy snake
That would dart
Along the scorching desert.

If only I could find
A beautiful butterfly
That would sweetly
Fly away in the flower meadow.

If only I could find
A darting dolphin
That would swim along
With me and be my friend.

Stephanie Willett (9)
Old Hall Junior School

The Roller-Roaring Tidal Wave

Calmly swaying like a rocking horse,
Swaying, side to side.
The breeze with a smile on its face
Was happily dancing around.

The little waves doing its job,
Bobbing up and down
As joyful as a Jack-in-the-box,
Jumping round and round.

Until the dreadful time had struck,
Chasing up and down,
The gigantic waves were no longer joyful
For the roller tidal wave.

At last the tidal wave was finally through,
Everything wrecked and demolished,
Nobody laughing any longer, just staring,
All just staring, like statues.

Samantha Harcourt (10)
Old Hall Junior School

The Storm

He started at dinner,
Knocking quite loudly.
Half a minute later it got worse
Banging violently.
Crash, bang, crash, bang,
We were the mice, he was the cat.
Raging around the house,
Twisting, roaring with all his might,
Banging furiously.
The sound goes down slowly . . . slowly, grey, blue
And then finally the sun.

Jasmine Hardy (9)
Old Hall Junior School

Wish Poem

If only I could find
A magical unicorn that could fly high
Above the blue sky.

If only I could find
A crab that could walk forwards
Not sideways!

If only I could find
A world full of people and animals
That would never die.

If only I could find
A place where it would be Christmas
Every day and my family will be with me.

If only I could find
A daft dog that could talk
I already have one, only she can't talk.

If only I could find
A brother and sister that aren't annoying
And would be nice to me.
That would be brilliant!

Olivia Doyle (9)
Old Hall Junior School

The Storm

He snarled his rage at teatime
I pretended I didn't care.
By bedtime he was screaming, tossing, turning,
My head started to ache.
He was becoming a pain.
In the morning, he was throwing dustbins.
Just try messing with a storm,
Even a tiny one!

Jonathon Dunn (10)
Old Hall Junior School

Wish Poem

If only I could find
A darting jaguar
That dashes everywhere.

If only I could find
A slithery snake
That slides and slithers all over.

If only I could find
A penny that would
Get anything I wanted.

If only I could find
A genius man that would
Help me with my maths.

If only I could find
A dancing dolphin
That would teach me how to dance.

If only I could find
A speedy spider
That could spin a web just like that!

Charlotte Machin (9)
Old Hall Junior School

The Storm

He started to roar at dinner time
By tea time he was worse.
He started to bang in furious rage.
At night-time I got scared,
In the morning, he started to throw fences.
I pretended I didn't care,
You try living through a giant storm
It's horrendous.

Robyn Canner (9)
Old Hall Junior School

Wish Poem

If only I could find
A fantastic fox
That flies forever.

If only I could find
A brilliant badger
That barks backwards.

If only I could find
A giant gorilla
That grants wishes.

If only I could find
A kicking kangaroo
That cooks cakes.

If only I could find
A careful cat
That counts in Spanish.

If only I could find
A brave bear
That borrows cuddly bears.

Abbie Layton (9)
Old Hall Junior School

The Storm

He started by calling names
I tried to walk away
At dinner time he was pushing me
Then I ran away
Next, he was throwing me around
I flew through the window
Cold, loud, twisting, banging
Just you try flying in a storm.

Robert Hepworth (9)
Old Hall Junior School

Cataract

Waiting in anticipation,
Crossing our fingers,
The nerve-racking suspense,
A fragile vase waiting to be broken.

Air rushing past our faces,
Like a jet in flight,
Dashed to pieces,
By the rocks, so jagged.

Swirling in spray,
Flying in foam,
Drowning in deep water.

The air that was thick with panic,
Filled with tranquillity,
Relief seeping everywhere,
Like a wave of happiness.

The waterfall had passed.

Georgina Layton (10)
Old Hall Junior School

The Storm

She whined just after tea time
I held my ears down
By bedtime she was vicious and
Shrieking with rage
I held my fingers in my ears
She was getting even stronger
And more powerful.
By that time she had calmed
Do not try this with a tornado
Especially with a little one!

Jack Wilson (9)
Old Hall Junior School

Wish Poem

If only I could find
A cloud that rains
Money when I want it to.

If only I could find
A dopey dog
That lives for 20 years.

If only I could find
A clever cat
That could help me with my homework.

If only I could find
A happy hamster
That could talk to me and be my friend.

If only I could find
A crazy crocodile
That could catch a cat.

If only I could find
A racy rat
That could race running rats.

Amy Carty (8)
Old Hall Junior School

Starry Night

The stars are glistening diamonds
In the night sky,
When the moon is full,
Anything is possible.
As the night goes on
The creatures creep.
The stars sparkle and start to fade
As the golden sun rises.

Molly Cannon (9)
Old Hall Junior School

Wish Poem

If only I could find
An amazing acrobat that
Could fly while he juggled.

If only I could find
A fantastic footballer that
Scored five goals every match.

If only I could find
A genius genie that could
Grant me a thousand wishes.

If only I could find
A fantastic Formula One car
That could speed down the road.

If only I could find
A pointy pencil that could whizz
Through my homework in half a second.

Jack Morton (8)
Old Hall Junior School

The Storm

She had a paddy at lunchtime
I just ignored her
By tea time she was roaring and banging
Later, she was a big pain
Getting more fierce by the hour
I got annoyed
Suddenly, she calmed down a lot
I was glad
Don't try it or else you'll get whirled
Up by the storm.

Jessica Dolling (10)
Old Hall Junior School

Wish Poem

If only I could find
A dopey dog
That lives forever.

If only I could find
A daft dragon
To take me everywhere.

If only I could find
A pretty princess
That would teach me to dance.

If only I could find
Everlasting Easter eggs
Then I would have chocolate for years.

If only I could find
A wonderful wardrobe
That could weave clothes.

If only I could find
A magical music box
That played my favourite tunes all day.

Emily Mason (8)
Old Hall Junior School

The Storm

He whined at breakfast,
I was so annoyed,
by lunchtime he was banging and roaring,
I pretended not to hear.
By teatime he was attacking me,
I was so annoyed,
try going out in a roaring, violent, angry storm
even a little one.

Daniel Lobar (9)
Old Hall Junior School

Wish Poem

If only I could find
A clever cat
That talks and shares secrets.

If only I could find
A singing snake
That goes on TV like an actor.

If only I could find
A flying fairy
That plays and grants me wishes.

If only I could find
A reading rabbit
That tells stories like a teacher.

If only I could find
A laughing lion
That tells me funny jokes.

If only I could find
An amazing angel
That is pretty and makes friends.

Eleanor Haughey (8)
Old Hall Junior School

The Storm

He was blowing mightily, twisting
burning, blazing
fierce as a Chinese Ninja
powerful yet quick
I try to stay away from him
he is too loud to bear
crashing, smashing through the school
don't risk a storm like this or you'll be
blown clean away.

Tyler Bonser (10)
Old Hall Junior School

Wish Poem

If only I could find
A beautiful butterfly
Whose wings glow in
The night sky to
Guide my way home.

If only I could find
A furious flea flitting
From fox to fox.

If only I could find
A curious cat that
Cooks cakes.

Eleanor Middleton (9)
Old Hall Junior School

Wish Poem

If only I could find
A flippy fish that could fly like a swooping skylark.

If only I could find
A prototype peregrine darting across the high hills.

If only I could find
A bold bald eagle prowling its land.

If only I could find
An odd old owl screeching in the moonlight.

If only I could find
An elegant heron strutting in the snow.

Edmund Austin (9)
Old Hall Junior School

Wish Poem

If only I could find
A delicious dessert
That tastes like chocolate
With ice cream that can
Last forever.

If only I could find
An ancient tennis racket
That gives me amazing
Tennis skills.

If only I could find
A Yu-Gi-Oh! card that
Is the greatest of all
And has super powers.

If only I could find
A magic remote control
That could take me
Into the TV.

If only I could find
A hover bike
That could transport me to
The lost city of Atlantis.

If only I could find
Jack's magic beans
To find the giant's treasure
Inside his castle.

Harry Large (9)
Old Hall Junior School

Wish Poem

If only I could find
A beautiful butterfly whose wings
Shine bright like fairy lights in the dark night sky.

If only I could find
A genius genie who would grant me my every wish
From a kangaroo to a shiny dish.

If only I could find
A marvellous mansion with Penelopy Princess sat inside
Who is as beautiful as a butterfly.

If only I could find
A dancing dolphin who could put on shows
And win me money to my heart's desire.

If only I could find
An enormous elephant
Who I could ride on high
And who would pick up logs and pull down trees.

Emily Calladine (9)
Old Hall Junior School

Wish Poem

If only I could find
The fastest Ferrari in the entire universe.

If only I could find
One million pounds of shiny amber.

If only I could find
Einstein's mathematics skills.

If only I could find
The most heavy thrash metal in the entire music charts.

Jacob Smith (9)
Old Hall Junior School

Wish Poem

If only I could find
The fastest flying, fantastic Ferrari
That speeds at over 500 miles per hour.

If only I could find
A fab footballer who
Scores a hat-trick at every match.

If only I could find
A colourful, cuddly kitten.

If only I could find
A dreadful dynamite to blow up my garden shed.

Niccòlo Ebong (8)
Old Hall Junior School

Wish Poem

If only I could find
A fantastic dog
Who could solve my problems.

If only I could find
A fantastic boot
Which could score 10 goals each game.

If only I could find
A lion which was
Mad from chocolate.

If only I could find
The FA football people
Who let me be a manager.

Oliver Naughton (8)
Old Hall Junior School

Wishing Poem

If only I could find
An enormous mansion filled
With sparkly new gold
Shining in my eyes.

If only I could find
A spectacular wishing
Genie to grant my every wish.

If only I could find
A speedy Volvo that
Shines all day long in the sun.

If only I could find
A sweet dream house
Filled with fluffy light hearts
Of my dreams.

If only I could find
My suitcase packed every week
For the best holiday ever
With the palm trees swaying.

If only I could find
Birthday presents at the
Bottom of my bed, more
Than once a year.

Nicola Hill (8)
Old Hall Junior School

D-Day

The sound of the landing craft,
The sight of the firing guns,
The smell of blood
And the taste of sand in my mouth
And the feeling of fear inside me.

Matthew Parker (11)
Redhill Primary School

My Cat

Her name was Penny,
She loved me so,
She was quite steady,
Soft and slow.

She would climb on my bed,
Every night,
Until dawn would come,
And make my bedroom light.

But one day,
We moved house,
She ran away,
I sat there waiting for her day after day.

I think of her,
In every way,
Hoping she'll come back one day.

Holly Riley (10)
Redhill Primary School

My Rabbit

I have a rabbit so sweet and soft.
I have a rabbit that is black and white.
I have a rabbit that I can stroke and hold.
I have a rabbit that is big and fat.

My rabbit is fast and cool.
My rabbit eats cabbage and carrots.
My rabbit loves me like I love him.
My rabbit likes to eat food.

My rabbit is the best.

Siobhan Wenham (11)
Redhill Primary School

Twinkling Stars In The Special Sky

Twinkling stars in the sky,
so bright you could look at them
and they would twinkle in your eyes.

Twinkle, twinkle, just so sweet,
the twinkle, twinkle, could smile in your eyes.

Twinkle, twinkle in the sky,
just so high I could touch them
twinkling in my dreams,
so high my friends could come with me
in my dreams.

Twinkle, twinkle, just in the sky,
I can hear the twinkle in the sky.

Twinkle, twinkle, here I go
in a rocket to see the twinkle in the sky.

Katie Louise Tatam (7)
Redhill Primary School

The Loneliness Of The Playground

The sound of the rustling leaves,
And the wind blowing through the trees,
Is all you can hear,
On the playground.

The sight of the field,
And the sun rising from the sky,
Is all you can see,
On the playground.

The touch of the morning sunlight
In your eyes,
And the feeling of sadness,
Is all you can feel
On the playground.

Jack Thompson (10)
Redhill Primary School

Boris

When Boris was small,
A cute little puppy,
He had big brown eyes,
And ears very fluffy.

But some years on,
He hardly ever got up,
Not like he used to
When he was a pup.

Then one day,
I rushed downstairs,
And I saw Boris,
Lying there.

My mum said
He was in a deep sleep.
So I opened one of his eyes,
To have a quick peep.

But the shine wasn't there
In his big brown eyes
So I sat next to him,
And began to cry.

Laura Clough (11)
Redhill Primary School

Devon

Devon is so much fun.
The caravan site is so big.
The beach is really great.
You can run up and down and play in the sand.
Back at the site there are children
Splashing in the pool.
The water is cold.

Kirsty Dakin (10)
Redhill Primary School

My Dad!

My dad is *so* cool
He goes to the allotment with me
He goes on bike rides with me
He watches TV with me
He even goes to the football stadium with me
I think my dad is *so* cool!

Hannah Brown (7)
Redhill Primary School

Playtime

Children sit and watch the clock tick.
It's time to have fun,
It's time to play,
Jump up, run,
Play a new game.
Hear children shouting, 'Come and play,
Taste the break you've brought today.'
The whistle goes,
The fun has ended,
Each class is called.

    Playtime has ended!

Sophie Webster (10)
Redhill Primary School

Expensive

The world is *expensive* in a way
Because you always have to pay
I wish that the world were a nice place
Because then every girl would have make-up on her face.
The world never stops
Because everywhere there are shops.

Josie Smith (8)
Redhill Primary School

Liverpool Fan At Anfield

L is for lovely smell of hot dogs.
I is for intelligent managers.
V is for Van Nistlerooy on the ball.
E is for everyone cheering, what a goal!
R is for Ronaldo's tricks.
P is for pasties at the big game.
O is for Oliver Kahn making a great save.
O is for orange on the advertising banners.
L is for Liverpool, the greatest team of them all.

F is for a foul on Raul.
A is for a substitution.
N is for nearly a goal.

A is for Arsenal, the Premiership holders.
T is for Tranmere in Coca Cola League One.

A is for Adriano, the golden boot winner.
N is for Norwich City's David Bentley.
F is for fighting in the crowd.
I is for international teams.
E is for England who are the best in the world.
L is for losers in the big game.
D is for Derby County.

Jamie Fenwick (11)
Redhill Primary School

My Hamster

H is for happy little hamster.
A is for amazing as he runs on his wheel.
M is for mischievous, he's good at that.
S is for his soft and silky fur.
T is for trouble, he's always in trouble.
E is for exciting, you just have to look at him.
R is for rascal, he's the biggest rascal there ever was.

But I've got to say he's the sweetest hamster in the world.

Vanessa Radford (11)
Redhill Primary School

Fluffy

I have a cat called Fluffy,
She is a tabby cat,
She sleeps in the day curled up on a mat.
I watch her in the garden,
Chasing birds and leaves
And when she gets tired,
She curls upon my knees.

Ellie May Lawson (8)
Redhill Primary School

Hearts

Hearts are smart
They play a very big part
In our lives when they start.
All hearts begin when you are born
And on your sleeve they can be worn.
You can hear your heart thumping and
Bump, bump, bumping.
There are many different kinds of hearts,
Smart hearts, greedy hearts,
Silly hearts, kind hearts, rude hearts.
I wonder what type of heart you have?

Elinor Hardcastle (8)
Redhill Primary School

Once There Was A Whale

Once there was a whale
Who got blown away by a gale
Then it started to hail
So it hid under its tail
Whilst it was doing so
It tried to eat a snail!
And it saw a fat man in jail.

Phoebe Garside (8)
Redhill Primary School

Swimming

Smell of chlorine and smoke from the gun.
'Wow!' goes the crowd and the fun has begun.
I'm so excited, I can't wait!
My swimming club is chanting madly.
My mouth takes a swallow.
It's time to jump off the block.
Now I'm off through the splashing water,
Goggles gripping my face.

Haydn Bowley (11)
Redhill Primary School

We've Got Some Pet Scaries!

My mother's got a troll, it helps around the house
And it's also good at eating next-door's nasty mouse.
My dad has a gargoyle that annoys my mum
But when it's naughty, it bites his sticky bum.
My sister has a goblin that tidies up her face
And when someone's going to hit her, it cracks its giant mace.
But I think their favourite pet of all is me
Their own pet trouble, but I'll annoy them all, you'll see!

Jack Hodgkinson (8)
Redhill Primary School

Hush Little Baby

'Hush little baby, please don't cry.'
He went to sleep with a sigh,
As he wakes up I'm the first he sees,
I held him in my arms as I looked for the keys,
We went for a ride in the car,
Then we went to the shops for a chocolate bar,
When we got home, I put him to bed,
'Go to sleep my little child,' I said.

Danielle Mortimer (11)
St Joseph's Catholic Primary School, Derby

The Seasons

Spring
Flowers growing,
Young lambs in the fields,
Jumping and dancing happily,
Spring.

Summer
Weather is great,
Holidays starting now,
People wearing shorts and T-shirts,
Summer.

Autumn
Bonfire Night,
Leaves start changing colour,
All the boys and girls wrap up warm,
Autumn.

Winter
Snow falls at night,
Everywhere is covered with snow,
People build snowmen on the ground,
Winter.

Natalie Bentley (11)
St Joseph's Catholic Primary School, Derby

Big Fear

Natalie lives outside an old theme park
Victorians used to go to.
She's terrified of it, she can't move flats
because no one would buy hers, it's too noisy.
Every night when it's dark she thinks everyone
who used to go there a long time ago is after her,
she can't close her eyes because they're still there,
she has nightmares about being killed in her own home.
That's Natalie's big fear!

Eleanor Balwako (10)
St Joseph's Catholic Primary School, Derby

It's A . . .

Mouse slayer,
Fish hater,
Mouse mauler,
Spider hauler,
Mouse chaser,
Real racer,
Dog's dinner,
Superb winner,
It's really fat,
It sleeps on a mat,
It's tall,
It's small,
It likes fish,
Eats out of a dish,
It drinks water,
Then goes out to slaughter,
It rhymes with hat

It's a . . . ?

Otis Gratton (10)
St Joseph's Catholic Primary School, Derby

The Winter Season

Snowflakes falling gently to the ground,
As graceful as a feather,
Not making a sound.

Frost creeps up the windowpane,
Spreading wide and tall,
Covering its way,
Like ivy up a wall.

When the little animals enjoy their hibernation,
Each in their cosy bed,
The geese set out on their emigration,
So their goslings can be fed.

Alice Iddon (10)
St Joseph's Catholic Primary School, Derby

Cinquain Poetry

Dog

> A dog,
> On a hot rock,
> Playing with other dogs,
> Licking, barking, fighting, playing,
> All day.

Shark

> White shark,
> Swimming along,
> In the freezing cold sea,
> Coming towards me to get me
> And kill.

Mark Durkan (10)
St Joseph's Catholic Primary School, Derby

Big Fears

Outside Jack's house,
On top of the same tree every night,
Sits a huge hawk,
Wailing, his blood-red eyes checking the area,
The cold not affecting him,
His shadow looming over the window.

Jack lies on his bed every night,
Hoping that the bird will disappear,
But he has more worries . . .
That the hawk will fly into his room
And start attacking him in his sleep.

Joe Koscinski (11)
St Joseph's Catholic Primary School, Derby

My Dad

My dad loves motorbikes
Motorbikes are what he likes
He has had 38
He must think they are really great!
Once he had a bad crash
And got covered in gravel rash.
He's always buying motorbike magazines
And leather jeans.
Dad thinks bikes are best by far,
But wishes he could just get a car.

My dad is crazy about motorbikes!

Paige Kathryn Smith (11)
St Joseph's Catholic Primary School, Derby

Uni-Dragon

Beware of its glowing eyes
They will turn you to stone
If you have a will of steel
You might survive alone.

The young man of Jacob said
'I will kill this dragon
No one can stop me
If I ride my lucky wagon.'

So he set off on his quest
Determined to find this beast
But sad to say, a sorry tale
The dragon had a feast!

Jacob Rollinson (10)
St Joseph's Catholic Primary School, Derby

It's A . . .

Fast hopper
furry body
lettuce eater
mover groover
fat tummy
little ears
little paws.
carries a basket.

It's a . . . ?

Bethany Masters (10)
St Joseph's Catholic Primary School, Derby

Pig - Cinquain

Pink pigs,
Small, muddy,
Their babies are so cute.
They are lazy, eat too much food.
Pink pigs.

Victoria Wyatt (11)
St Joseph's Catholic Primary School, Derby

It's A . . .

Mouse chaser
bird eater
dog hater
fish killer
fast runner
water hater
lazy crater
sometimes fat.

It's a . . . cat!

Fawn Quick (11)
St Joseph's Catholic Primary School, Derby

It's A . . .

Bird catcher
Pigeon slayer
Mouse chaser
Road racer
Wool player
Women's neighbour
Fish eater
Child entertainer
Fur leaver
Dog teaser
It sleeps on a mat

It's a . . . ?

Lauren Finnegan (10)
St Joseph's Catholic Primary School, Derby

It's A . . .

Mouse chaser
rat facer
fast mover
garden groover
sometimes tall
often small
pointy ears
not many fears
nice tail
not always male
nice to pat.

It's a . . . ?

James Durkan (10)
St Joseph's Catholic Primary School, Derby

Big Fears

Outside Tom's room,
Opposite his window is another boy's room,
This boy keeps a big box of spiders,
Sometimes the spiders scuttle across the window sill.

Tom lies awake in bed at night,
He feels as if spiders are all over him,
He can see spiders in the dark,
And he has to hide under the blanket.

This is Tom's *big fear!*

Emma Joyce (10)
St Joseph's Catholic Primary School, Derby

Nagging

'Don't let out the cat,
Fetch your hat,
Don't be cheeky,
Turn off the TV,
Close the door,
Clean the floor,
Don't rest,
Get dressed,
Let out the dog,
Beware of the fog.

Go and get your bag ready,
Don't run, go steady,
Do your tie,
Say goodbye,
Turn off the light,
Say goodnight.'

Chloe Knowles (10)
St Peter & St Paul School, Chesterfield

Parents Like You To . . .

Watch your manners,
Be polite,
Get up early,
Switch off your light.
Have a wash,
Polish your shoes,
Clean the lounge,
Watch your Ps and Qs.
Wash the car,
Never swear,
Not eat too many sweets,
Comb your hair.
Do well at school,
Go to sleep,
Eat your fruit,
Wipe your feet.

Georgia Stansbury (9)
St Peter & St Paul School, Chesterfield

Parents Like You To . . .

Be good boys,
never swear,
tidy your toys,
brush your hair,
set the table,
be polite,
tell your brother a fable,
turn out the light,
clean the shower,
don't weep,
don't slouch down low,
go to sleep!

James Davies (10)
St Peter & St Paul School, Chesterfield

What I Dread To Hear . . .

'Start to obey,
Sit down,
Don't eat as a clown,
You drive or we're not going,
What do you mean, you're not sewing?
Set the table,
What about Mabel?
Close the door,
Be in by four,
Be polite,
Sometimes fight,
You're never right.

Wash your hands,
Don't forget the pans,
Never commit crimes,
Always rhyme,
We're going on a journey,
We need to pick up Emily.

Don't slurp,
Try not to burp,
Cook dinner
Or make me thinner,
Never lie,
Make me a pie.'

Sam Mather (9)
St Peter & St Paul School, Chesterfield

Parents Like You To; Parents Would Never Say

Parents like you to . . .
Do your homework,
Be polite,
Tidy your toys,
And never fight.

Not argue,
Go to bed,
Have a bath,
That's what I dread.

Brush your teeth,
Not snack before meals,
Not break things,
What an ordeal!

Not mess in the house,
Wipe your feet,
Don't talk from a different room,
Go to sleep.

Be kind,
Do not swear,
Take your elbows off the table,
Brush your hair.'

Parents would never say . . .
Eat all the chocolate,
Watch hours of TV,
Stay up all night,
Here's an iced coffee.

I'll do your homework,
Here's a hundred pounds,
I'll take you to the Trafford Centre,
Our favourite stomping ground.

Watch all the soaps dear,
Wear anything to school,
Have a friend over most nights dear
Make your own set of rules.

Katherine Parkin (9)
St Peter & St Paul School, Chesterfield

My Jammy Newsbook

Last night my mum was really cross.
Then she said that she was the boss,
And threw a tart at my brother Ross.
Ross lost his temper,
With my mother
And swiftly fired one back at her.
My mother thought
It was my sister,
Threw two at her
But strangely, missed her.
She threw four at Ross
And one at me!
I'm beginning to see
That she thinks it's me!
Throwing jam tarts is such thirsty work,
Never mind, it's time for tea!

Laura Singleton (9)
St Peter & St Paul School, Chesterfield

Parents Like You To . . .

Stop it,
Be quiet,
Never swear,
Be polite
And stroke my hair.

Tidy your room,
Turn off the tap,
Fetch a spoon
And get a snack.

Clean your plate,
Flush the toilet,
Not be late,
Have a bath,
Not wake up on a weekend.

Alexander Hodgkinson (9)
St Peter & St Paul School, Chesterfield

Parents Like You To . . .

Clean your teeth,
Not be rude,
Do your homework,
Tidy your room.

Get ready for school,
Not answer back,
Run down to the postbox,
Carry that.

Not pick your nose,
Brush your teeth,
Hurry up,
Not go in there.

Not have a tantrum,
Be polite,
Mind your manners,
Switch off the light.

Rebecca Bayliff (9)
St Peter & St Paul School, Chesterfield

I Would Like To Hear My Parents Say . . .

'You can do it later,
Stay up later.

Go into town,
I'll give you five pounds.

You can stay out as long as you want,
How much more money do you want?

Watch TV when you like,
Why don't you play with Mike?

I'll do the chores, play outside,
Don't work, relax.'

Callum Howie (10)
St Peter & St Paul School, Chesterfield

I Want My Mum To . . .

Not get me up,
Clean my muck,
Make my bed,
Let me play instead.
Take the dog for a walk,
Let me stay and talk,
Tidy my room
Let me hum my tune.
Brush my hair,
Not stand and stare,
Get me my dinner,
Make my drink a brimmer.
Let me watch telly,
Tickle my belly,
Not make me eat greens,
Fold away my jeans.
Switch off the light,
Say goodnight,
Let me watch the moon,
(Morning will come soon).

Lewis Spencer (10)
St Peter & St Paul School, Chesterfield

Parents Like You To . . .

Tidy your room,
Use the broom,
Brush your teeth,
Eat your beef,
Clean your plate,
Not be in late,
Put your clothes away,
Obey,
Not be bossy,
Not look too glossy.

Siân Carter (9)
St Peter & St Paul School, Chesterfield

Parents Like You To . . .

Watch your manners,
Be polite,
Remember your w's,
Put the wood in the hole,
Watch your Ps and Qs,
Go to the toilet,
Never swear or
Give people a fright,
Switch off the light,
Eat your greens,
Be quiet for five minutes,
Do your homework,
Not talk with your mouth full,
Set the table,
Read a book.

Richard Berry (10)
St Peter & St Paul School, Chesterfield

Food Newsbook

Last night my mum was really sad,
My brother ripped up my homework and went mad.
Dad came in as drunk as a bat,
And threw a Barbie doll on his hat.
I thought I would start a food fight for fun,
But then the trouble really began.
Spaghetti was thrown about,
So was Mum's freshly cooked trout!
Then all of us went terribly red
And starting throwing lumps of bread.
My sister threw two at me,
But somehow hit the old oak tree,
Then Mum was full of rage
And Dad, to keep Mum from fighting,
Trapped her in a secure metal cage.

Simon Meikle (8)
St Peter & St Paul School, Chesterfield

Parents Like You To . . .

Watch your manners,
Be polite,
Close your curtains,
Switch off the light,
Wash the dishes,
Fold your clothes,
Brush your teeth,
Not wake them up!
Not feed the fish too much,
Shut the cupboard,
Never answer back,
Eat with your mouth shut,
Turn you PS2 off!
Wave to your dad,
Never scream,
Wash your face,
Not blame your sister,
Not slam the door,
Not let the cat in,
See your dad.

Guy Swales (9)
St Peter & St Paul School, Chesterfield

Crazy Newsbook
(Based on 'Emma Hackett's Newsbook' by Allan Ahlberg)

Last night my mate got really mad,
And threw a potato at my dad.
My mum was snuggled up by the fire,
When Dad tripped up, Mum joined the choir.
My brother shouted out to me,
'Mary, make me a cup of tea.'
My mum couldn't hold her temper in,
And threw my brother in the bin!
Dad was chasing after me,
I rolled over and Dad went *'Whee!'*

Mary-Beth Owen (9)
St Peter & St Paul School, Chesterfield

Parents Like You To . . .

Watch your manners,
Be polite,
Get dressed,
Switch off the light.
Clean your teeth,
Polish your shoes,
Go and play,
Watch your Ps and Qs.
Go to school,
Never swear,
Speak up,
Comb your hair.
Be quiet,
Go to sleep,
Play a game with your sister,
Wipe your feet.
Turn down that racket,
Shut up!

James Rowland (10)
St Peter & St Paul School, Chesterfield

Parents Like You To . . .

Watch your manners,
Be polite,
Tidy your room,
Fetch the broom,
Not play with your food,
Get out of that mood.
Set the table,
Not upset Mabel,
Not slam the door,
Be in by four!

Charlotte Adams (10)
St Peter & St Paul School, Chesterfield

Parents Like You To . . .

Watch your manners,
Say 'Please' and 'Thank you',
Shut up!
Sleep the right way up,
Stop messing about!
Be quiet,
Behave!
I thought I said no TV,
Say 'Sorry',
Wash your hair,
Tidy your room,
Sit up smartly,
Get out of bed,
Switch off the light,
Wipe your feet,
Stop playing.

Edward Richardson (9)
St Peter & St Paul School, Chesterfield

Bryony's Newsbook
(Based on 'Emma Hackett's Newsbook' by Allan Ahlberg)

Last night my mum got really sad,
Then aimed some ice cream at my dad.
The ice cream landed on Dad's back,
So he chucked some jam tarts in a sack.
Dad fired the sack at my mum,
Who was holding the baby sucking its thumb.
The baby who is only four,
Threw a cake at Mum and hit the door.
My sister got really mad,
Then threw a Swiss roll at Chad.
Chad threw an ice cream at my brother,
Who ducked down, then it smacked my mother.
My mum finally got fed up,
And poured some milk into a cup.

Bryony Hill (8)
St Peter & St Paul School, Chesterfield

Chocolatey Newsbook
(Based on 'Emma Hackett's Newsbook' by Allan Ahlberg)

Last night
I got really mad,
And threw my homework
At my dad,
My dad scrunched
My homework up,
And put it in the china cup.
My mum joined in
And threw a pile of
Work papers in the bin,
Then my brother
Had some fun,
And threw a chocolate cake
At my mum!
But somehow missed her
And the crumbled cake
Whacked my sister!

Erin Hawker (9)
St Peter & St Paul School, Chesterfield

Parents Like You To . . .

Watch your manners,
Be polite,
Clean your room,
Switch off the light,
Polish the dishes,
Shine your shoes,
Be nice,
Watch your Ps and Qs,
Kiss your mum,
Never swear,
Eat your dinner,
Go to sleep,
Not be bad.

James Watson (9)
St Peter & St Paul School, Chesterfield

Crushed-Up Apples
(Based on 'Emma Hackett's Newsbook' by Allan Ahlberg)

Last night my mother
Got really crazy,
And threw an apple
At my friend Daisy.
Daisy lost her temper
With my mother,
Threw one at me
But somehow missed me.
Then my sister,
Thinking it was me,
Hurled two at me.
Then the baby had some fun
And threw her dummy
At Daisy's mummy.
Daisy howled, 'Don't do that!'
In a voice so loud,
She frightened the cat!

Ellie Birch (9)
St Peter & St Paul School, Chesterfield

Nagging

'Go out and play,
have a good day.
Check what the football score is,
it could be our big chance today.
Stop trying to annoy your sister,
my dad shouts, *'We've won, hooray!'*
Go and get changed, we're going to the pub,
but if you want to come, you'd better be good.

Don't ask silly questions, you're wasting time,
don't slam the door or you'll be having an early night.
Tidy your room, get ready for bed,
don't be noisy or I'll take away your precious ted.'

Amber Richardson (9)
St Peter & St Paul School, Chesterfield

Parents Like You To . . .

Brush your teeth,
Wash your face,
Put up the wreath.
Never swear,
Tidy your room,
Comb your hair.
Take the dogs for a walk,
Pick up Sam's cup,
Never talk.
Not leave your shoes on the floor,
Hang your coat up,
Close the door.
Feed the hamster,
Put your plate in the kitchen,
Check on the dog.
Pack your bag,
Turn off the light,
Go to bed!

Laura Hattersley (9)
St Peter & St Paul School, Chesterfield

My Special Newsbook
(Based on 'Emma Hackett's Newsbook' by Allan Ahlberg)

Last night my dad became really dumb,
He threw a jam tart at my mum.
Mum lost her temper,
Then with Dad,
Who threw another at her
And hit our dog, poor Lad.
Poor Lad thought it was my sister,
And threw four at her
But somehow missed her.
My sister, only three,
Hurled four at poor Lad
And twenty at me!
My friend's brother, only three,
Threw two at Mum
And ten at me.
Mum had had enough,
So she shouted, 'Time for tea!'
Everyone ran, and fell on me!

Sara Sinclair (8)
St Peter & St Paul School, Chesterfield

Winter

The dull grey sky
Covers hills of snow,
Where the trees are silent,
Standing bare in the fields.

The church lies in the trees,
Funny-shaped white fields,
The trees move in the wind,
All is blank and bare.

The river flows smoothly,
Flowing through the land.
It's so clean you can see in it,
By the bank, weeds grow in the water.

Patrick Field (9)
St Wystan's School, Repton

Winter

The frostbitten trees in the sky,
Slowly wave as the wind whistles by,
The birds fluff up their feathers to keep warm,
And shelter from the gathering storm.

Hidden in the valley lies a church,
Square tower pointing to the sky,
Pheasants fly in to feed,
Scratching frantically to uncover seed.

A dog walk becomes a polar exploration,
Cold paws padding on freezing ice,
Wet nose quivers in the cold,
Or is it excitement with which he quivers?

The church tower reflects the hour,
Shining in the sickly sun,
Standing straight and tall, it beckons all,
To the village, home, hearth and fire.

Peter Bralesford (9)
St Wystan's School, Repton

Winter

When the sky is grey,
The forest is bleak,
Bare trees are hollow,
Dusted in snow.

When the village is quiet,
So cosy and sweet,
The houses are warm,
Glowing fires give it heat.

Ducks nestle in the snow,
The cows shelter behind the hedge,
Chickens scratch around for food
As the light begins to fade.

David Boiling (9)
St Wystan's School, Repton

The Workhouse

The workhouse,
A horrible place to be,
Scary, slavery, terrible.
As silent as a grave,
As grey as a pavement,
Glad I wasn't there,
As glad as a lottery winner.
The workhouse,
A home for the poor.

The workhouse,
A place of horror and misery,
Miserable, dark, musty.
As lifeless as a stone,
As dark as the night sky.
Sorry for the people who were there,
As sorry as a mourner at a grave.
The workhouse,
A prison for the homeless.

Aimee Holder-Spinks (10)
St Wystan's School, Repton

Winter

Snow drifts down,
Onto the rooftops.
The snow comes from
The dark rainy sky.

Brick-red houses
Line the street.
People singing carols
On the doorsteps.

People making footprints
On the white blanket of snow.
Children unwrapping presents
From Santa and the reindeer.

Richard Sommerville (9)
St Wystan's School, Repton

Queen Victoria

Queen Victoria.
She was born in 1819.
Powerful, rich and grand.
As grand as a swan.
As powerful as a superhero.
I feel weak compared to her.
As weak as a baby.
Queen Victoria.
The way she made Britain powerful.

Queen Victoria.
She ruled Britain for 64 years.
Proud, gracious and magnificent.
As proud as an inventor.
As magnificent as an angel.
I feel small.
As small as an ant.
Queen Victoria.
She changed the world.

Robert Egan (11)
St Wystan's School, Repton

Winter

The sky hangs overhead, bleak and empty.
A white and grey canvas for winter.
The wind whips and lashes the groaning trees.
Its crispy and icy bite freezes everything it touches.

The houses, covered in glimmering snow.
Pointed icicles hang from roofs,
The trees shiver, blown by the freezing wind,
The bushes are tinged with white.

Trudging men lead their chilly sheep in for the winter,
The sheep shiver from the cold, their fleeces covered in white.
The shepherds think of warm fire and cosy houses,
Hurrying their sheep through the winter's snow.

Oliver Startin (10)
St Wystan's School, Repton

Cars

Cars,
They were invented in Victorian times,
Beautiful, fast, amazing.
They whip past you like a flying eagle,
Their shining paint is as smooth as cream.
They're a wonderful invention,
As wonderful as the sunset, it's shocking to see them go.
Cars,
Something magical and wonderful.

Cars,
They started slow but increased in speed,
Elegant, posh, noisy.
As beautiful as a swan,
As noisy as a football crowd.
Amazed at the engineering,
As amazing as the ocean.
Cars,
A magnificent ride in the country.

Sophie Donoghue (11)
St Wystan's School, Repton

Winter

The sky is a steely blue,
Canadian geese go flying through.
The clouds are drifting by,
An icy wind passes with a sigh.

Evergreen trees glisten with frost,
Footprints in the snow where the cattle have crossed.
Sheep are cosily huddled together,
Glad of their fleeces in this chilly weather.

There are people playing in the snow,
A river so frozen it will not flow.
The ground is covered in a veil of white,
People walking in the morning light.

Liam Rhatigan (10)
St Wystan's School, Repton

Florence Nightingale

Florence Nightingale,
A carer to the wounded soldiers,
Loving, caring, kind,
As caring as a mother,
As graceful as a ballerina,
A very helpful lady,
As helpful as a doctor,
She is Florence Nightingale,
A mother to us all.

Florence Nightingale,
A woman who could soothe the poor,
Beautiful, elegant, graceful,
As beautiful as a bluebird,
As elegant as a swan,
A really wonderful woman,
As wonderful as a parent,
She is Florence Nightingale,
The Lady of the Lamp.

Holly Twells (11)
St Wystan's School, Repton

Winter

The grey gloomy sky,
Like a sea of cotton wool,
Tinged with yellow paint,
Snow clouds hanging in the sky.

The faraway hills,
With their blankets of snow,
Shiver and glimmer in the daylight,
Shining with a purple glow.

Shadows flicker on the white, frosty road,
As the sunshine pierces the broken hedge,
Their stripes glowing on the icy road,
Like a winter zebra crossing.

Eleanor Harrison (9)
St Wystan's School, Repton

Queen Victoria

Queen Victoria
She was Queen from 1837-1901
She was very royal, magnificent and graceful.
Regal, like an ocean liner on the waves
Like a calm tiger ready to pounce
You make me feel proud.
As proud as a peacock,
Queen Victoria
She was the ruler of the Empire.

Queen Victoria
She lived from 1819-1901,
She was elegant, proud and wonderful.
Dressed as black as the ace of spades
She was as elegant as a swan.
It makes me feel great that someone cared
As great as St Nicholas himself.
Queen Victoria
She was The Queen who made Britain great!

Oliver Richards (10)
St Wystan's School, Repton

Winter

The sky is a light blue,
With birds flying up high.
Glistening snow drifting from above,
Scattering across the ground.

The rooftops are covered by snow,
Carol singers singing under the bus shelter.
Windows opening and closing,
Chimneys are puffing with smoke.

People carrying logs for the fire,
Horses and carts trotting through the snow.
Bare trees swaying in the wind,
Happy children playing in the snow.

Chloe Marshall (10)
St Wystan's School, Repton

Queen Victoria

Queen Victoria,
She was born in 1819,
Magnificent, wonderful and beautiful.
As elegant as a ballerina,
As gracious as a swan.
She made a magnificent Queen in British history,
A caring mother for England.
Queen Victoria,
The longest serving Queen.

She was crowned in 1837,
Loving, amazing and gracious.
As pretty as a picture,
As proud as a peacock.
She was a powerful ruler,
As powerful as a steam engine.
Queen Victoria,
A lady of true royalty.

Harriet Boyles (11)
St Wystan's School, Repton

Winter

A cold winter's day,
With the sun piercing the clouds.
Brooding on a village,
Silent but deadly.

Houses stand tall,
Covered in snow.
Trees in the distance,
On a lonely hill.

People gather outside,
Walking, talking or skating.
White snow glitters,
Soft underfoot.

Philippa Stazicker (9)
St Wystan's School, Repton

The Crimean War

The Crimean War.
France, Britain and Sardinia versus Russia
It was a silly bloody war.
It was like a stopper on life.
I feel pity for the people.
Like a child to a dead bird.
The Crimean War.
The massacre of the charge of the Light Brigade.

The Crimean War.
Happened because Russia invaded Turkey.
Heroic, evil and cruel.
Like an explosion of snow.
A snapshot of Hell.
Despair at the loss.
As black as a starless night.
The Crimean War.
Victory at a huge cost.

Thomas Jones (12)
St Wystan's School, Repton

Winter

The holly trees blow in the wind,
They slowly move from side to side.
All the snow falls to the ground,
The leaves are green and prickly.

The postbox hangs on a wooden post,
Its top all covered with snow,
Tall grasses grow up the side,
Gently blowing in the wind.

A robin is perched on the postbox,
It has snow round its feet.
With his red bib and brown coat,
He sits and whistles a merry tune.

Holly Wright (9)
St Wystan's School, Repton

Queen Victoria

Queen Victoria,
Ruled 1837 to 1901.
Graceful, just and wise.
As wise as an owl,
As graceful as a swan.
She makes me proud,
Queen Victoria,
The British Empire.

Queen Victoria,
Married Albert in 1840.
Loving, kind and powerful.
As loving as a mother,
As powerful as her Empire.
I'm glad she was Queen,
Like a flower greeting the rain.
Queen Victoria,
She changed the world.

Emily Hammond (11)
St Wystan's School, Repton

Winter

The moon glimmers in the dark sky,
It shines through the night,
Like a torch in the dark,
A large white ball in a sea of grey.

The deep, dark woods in the gloom,
The trees sway in the freezing winds,
All is silent apart from the hoot of an owl,
The hills shine silver in the distance.

The grass is covered by waves of white snow,
Tufts of grass pierce the blanket of white.
Shadows loom across the thickening dusk.
The owl perches silently watching for movement.

Charlotte Downs (9)
St Wystan's School, Repton

The Great Exhibition

You were built in 1851
You are mighty, tall and awesome
As vast as a mountain
As large as a pyramid
You make me feel small
Like a bear compared to an ant
The Great Exhibition
A masterpiece of cast iron and glass.

The Great Exhibition
You were built by Prince Albert
Large, impressive and amazing
As solid as a rock
As transparent as ice
It makes me feel proud
As proud as a peacock
The great Exhibition
A wonderful feat of engineering.

Victor Scattergood (11)
St Wystan's School, Repton

Steam Train

The first horseless carriage.
As fast as a falcon.
Fast, elegant, steaming.
As long as a road.
I feel proud.
Proud as a peacock.
Steam trains.
A life-changing invention.

Steam trains,
A glorious invention.
Wonderful, fantastic, awesome.
As big as a building,
As posh as a duke.
I feel amazed.
Amazed as a clown.
Steam trains.
A fantastic device.

Tristan Griffiths (10)
St Wystan's School, Repton

Queen Victoria

Victoria, Queen of 19th century England
Was powerful, mighty and wonderful
She was as mighty as a lion
But, like a swan, she was graceful
She abolished the red flag law
And made the townsfolk and I happy.
Queen Victoria reminds me
How great the kings and queens are.

Queen Victoria, wife of Prince Albert
Was grateful, magnificent and proud.
As beautiful as a swan
And as famous as a god.
Thankful that she abolished the red flag law
As proud as a peacock,
Queen Victoria reminds me
How great the Victorians were.

Matthew Cort (11)
St Wystan's School, Repton

Winter

The sky is dark and gloomy,
The chilly wind grips me tight.
The bleak sun is slowly setting,
And I fear the sharp wind's bite.

All the frozen trees are bare
The newly fallen snow lies on the ground.
The wet branches wave about,
Frosty winter is all around.

Trudging back through crispy snow,
My footprints trailing behind me.
Thinking of the home fire, glowing bright
With hot buttered toast for tea.

Hollie Strong (10)
St Wystan's School, Repton

Queen Victoria

She became Queen at 18,
Magnificent, vile and strong.
As elegant as a swan,
As pretty as a picture.
She made a wonderful queen,
Like a sweet-smelling rose.
Queen Victoria,
The world is a wonderful place.

Queen Victoria,
She died in 1901.
Beautiful, loving and amazing,
As graceful as a bird.
As proud as a peacock,
I am glad she was Queen.
As grateful as a pauper,
Queen Victoria.
She was a very powerful lady.

Jessica Storey (10)
St Wystan's School, Repton

My Best Goal

I take the ball round the midfield,
People chanting my name,
Concentrate, concentrate!
That's all that's flashing through my head.
I twist round defence,
Only the keeper to beat.
The keeper dives.
It goes through his legs.
The whole crowd stands up and shouts.
I do a front flip, hug my mates,
It's the best feeling you can have.

George Lee (9)
Thornsett Primary School

Stray Cat

I walk around a city,
Underneath the street lights.
I walk past the flats,
By the offices and the houses.

A rattle in a bin,
A figure in the alleyway,
A howl in the wind,
A burglar in a flat.

I see another stray cat,
It hisses at me and springs,
I dodge its claws,
Its eyes fierce, I run away.

A footstep out of nowhere,
The call of a crow,
The engine of a car,
The chime of Big Ben.

Arms grab me,
They take me to a house.
I skitter across floorboards,
I sit in front of a fire.

The crackle of the stove,
Friendly voices talking,
The purr of a cat,
My first friend.

We sit beside each other,
I sleep with her for hours.
Our owners give us milk,
And stroke our furry backs.

There's no sound,
There's only peace.

Olivia Ashley (10)
Thornsett Primary School

Bird's Perspective

The take-off from the tree,
The spreading of my wings,
I ascend from the safety of my home
Towards the land of death.

I spiral in the sky,
Dodge between the clouds,
See the lights below
Like thousands of cruel eyes.

I dive lower and see the toxic smoke,
Polluting my land of peace.
I see the rush of killing machines
On their long, straight roads.

Poor old badger, limp and lifeless,
Killed by the hunter's gun.
The dirt and rubbish,
Floating through the streets.

I land in a square, people kick and shoo me.
I fly to a church, I find no peace in there.
They whack me, throw their human filth.
I leap into the air, skim the broken roof.

I go as fast as I can,
Leave the city far behind.
To my home I fly,
To the safety of my tree.

They should have left it to us birds,
But there's nothing we can do.
I prepare for another day of hatred,
As I fly, I think of what humans have done,
They have wasted this world of natural beauty.

Owen Baldwin (11)
Thornsett Primary School

On The Run

On the run
Where will I go?
Running away
I'm trembling with fear.

Hiding in an alleyway
Where will I go?
Is it all worth it?
I'm trembling with fear.

Eating scraps
Where will I go?
The police on my tail
I'm trembling with fear.

On my shoulder I feel a hand
'Come with me,' a policeman says.
What have I done?
I'm trembling with fear.

Iain Barr (9)
Thornsett Primary School

The Match

The players run down the tunnel,
The red, white and blue reflects in the light,
The crowds cheering at the sight,
The ball is kicked at full power,
Some say it'll reach Blackpool Tower!
Up and down goes the Mexican wave,
People say that tackle was brave,
They fear the opponent as they kick the ball,
They run up and stand tall,
The ref blows for full-time,
The players played divine.

Kieran Hopley (10)
Thornsett Primary School

The River

Narrow and cold
Winding and shallow
That's how the river begins.

Crashing and deep
Thundering and powerful
The river moves on.

Slow and winding
Wide and strong
This is the end of the river.

Tearfully we wave goodbye
As the river joins the sea
But don't worry,
We'll see him again.

Poppy Philligreen (9)
Thornsett Primary School

The Pencil In My Hand

The pencil in my hand is not in much use,
I'm trying to write things down,
But things just aren't coming out,
My mind is blank,
Time's tick-tocking away,
I'd better finish this essay.
I look at the clock,
It's half-past eight,
My work's not finished and it's getting late.
I'm trying to find excuses,
Like there's a history programme on ITV.
Ah! Suddenly words are in my head,
But what's that noise, 'Nicola, it's time for bed.'

Nicola Kemp (10)
Thornsett Primary School

A World Of Litter

Broken bottles like dangerous zigzags lying on the floor.
Plastic bags floating like ghosts.
Crisp packets like a rainbow in the sky.
Sweet wrappers shining in the sun.
Newspapers like big white butterflies.
Milkshake bottles make rattling sounds
As the wind blows them along the pavement.

Reece Jennings (7)
Thornsett Primary School

The River Journey

Cold, clear as crystal,
Bubbling and powerful,
The river begins its journey,
Swishing along the riverbed.
Cascading, crashing, thundering over waterfalls
And over rapids.
Now pouring and peaceful,
Slowing and silent,
Relaxing on its way to meet the sea.
It moves on, different shapes form,
The river becomes a sea.

Bethany Finch (9)
Thornsett Primary School

A World Of Litter

Crisp packets shining like stars in the night.
Ice pop wrappers floating in the air like dancing snakes.
Pieces of paper blowing wildly in the breeze.
Plastic bags land in the trees like owls.
Bottles smashing in the road.
My world of litter.

Emilie Lee (7)
Thornsett Primary School

A World Of Litter

Plastic bags cling to the trees like white doves.
Toffee wrappers blow around like witches on Hallowe'en.
Chip papers wave like flags in a hurricane.
Pepsi cans roll around sounding like unhappy ghosts.
A world of litter.

Daniella Gabbott (7)
Thornsett Primary School

Global Warming

It's icy and cold,
The whiteness of the snow really bold.
The frozen waste,
Skating penguins seem to race.
Shivers down my spine,
Global warming isn't fine.
All this beautiful scenery,
Is going to be ruined by diesel and machinery.
It's not going to be icy and cold,
The whiteness of the snow won't be bold.
The watery waste,
Skating penguins seeming not to race.
This is sending shivers down my spine,
Global warming is not fine!

Katy Waddell (11)
Thornsett Primary School

The She Wolf

She howls to the moonlight in the darkest night.
She lives in a cave, she is very brave.
She has a wolf friend that she will follow to the end.
She wails for his return, lying in the fern
Till the beast arrives - she hopes he survives!
She lies down to rest in her comfy nest.

Olivia Haslam (10)
Wigley Primary School

Spring

Little lambs skip in the meadows green.
Pink frilly blossom on luscious trees.
Daffodils bloom in little clumps.
Water in the brook tinkles over stones.
Fluffy yellow chicks hatch out of eggs.
Bees hover over flowers.
Sun shines out of Heaven's high bower.
I love spring.

Kate Walker (10)
Wigley Primary School

Monkey - Haiku

A little monkey
There he goes - swinging madness
Funny little chimp.

Jack Boughey (10)
Wigley Primary School

Knight

Pushed aside by others
Too weak to play
Won't swim with others
Scared away
Didn't know why
Just found out
Saw him trying on earrings, pearl
That weak knight is a girl!

Rebecca Hannon (10)
Wigley Primary School